Email This!

A Compilation of Humorous Emails and Anecdotes

J.D. Heskin

J.D. Heskin

DEDICATION

This book is dedicated to all the friends and family who shared with me these funny and heartwarming emails. It is also dedicated to the genius wit of all those who generated these great words and ideas over the years.

J.D. Heskin

CONTENTS

J.D. Heskin

Aging

A Little Gas

A little old lady goes to the doctor and says, "Doctor, I have this problem with gas. I fart all the time; although I must say, they never smell and are always silent. As a matter of fact, I've farted at least 20 times since I've been here in your office -- whoops, there goes another one! You didn't know I was farting, though, because they don't smell and are silent." The doctor says, "I see; here, take these pills and come back to see me in a week. The next week the old lady comes back. Doctor," she says, "I don't know what the heck you gave me, but now my farts, although still silent, stink terribly." The doctor says, "Good!!! Now that we've cleared up your sinuses, let's work on your hearing."

Hot Mama

A 92 year-old man went to the doctor to get a physical. A few days later, the doctor saw the man walking down the street with a gorgeous young lady on his arm. A couple of days later, when the old man had an appointment with the doctor again, the doc said, "You're really doing great, aren't you?" The man replied, "Just doing what you said doctor, 'Get a hot mamma and be cheerful'." The doctor said, "I didn't say that. I said you got a heart murmur. Be careful."

Mable's Anatomy

Mable was a 93 year-old woman who was particularly despondent over the recent death of her husband Harold. She decided that she would just kill herself and join him in death. Thinking that it would be best to get it over with quickly, she took out Harold's old Army pistol and made the decision to shoot herself in the heart since it was so badly broken in the first place. Not wanting to miss the vital organ and become a vegetable and burden to someone, she called her doctor's office to inquire as to just exactly where the heart would be. "On a woman," the doctor said, "your heart would be just below your left breast." Later that night, Mable was treated for a gunshot wound to her left kneecap.

The New Hearing Aid

Seems an elderly gentleman had serious hearing problems for a number of years. He went to the doctor and the doctor was able to have him fitted for a set of hearing aids that allowed the gentleman to hear 100%. The elderly gentleman went back in a month to the doctor and the doctor said, "Your hearing is perfect. Your family must be really pleased that you can hear again." To which the gentleman said, "Oh, I haven't told my family yet. I just sit around and listen to the conversations. I've changed my will three times!"

How To Know You're Getting Old

You're asleep, but others worry that you're dead.
Your back goes out more than you do.
You quit trying to hold your stomach in, no matter who walks into the room.
You buy a compass for the dash of your car.
You are proud of your lawn mower.
Your best friend is dating someone half their age and isn't breaking any laws.
You sing along with the elevator music.
You would rather go to work than stay home sick.
You constantly talk about the price of gasoline.
You enjoy hearing about other people's operations.
You consider coffee one of the most important things in life.
You make an appointment to see the dentist.
You no longer think of speed limits as a challenge.
Neighbors borrow YOUR tools.
People call at 9 p.m. and ask, "Did I wake you ?"
You have a dream about prunes.
You answer a question with, "because I said so!"
You send money to PBS.
The end of your tie doesn't come anywhere near the top of your pants.
You take a metal detector to the beach.
You wear black socks with sandals.
You know what the word "equity" means.
You can't remember the last time you laid on the floor to watch television.
Your ears are hairier than your head.
You get into a heated argument about pension plans.
You got cable for the weather channel.
You can go bowling without drinking.
You have a party and the neighbors don't even realize it.

An Old Cowhand

An old cowhand working on a ranch in Wyoming wants to go to the city. He draws his pay and gets a Greyhound ticket and rides to Omaha. He thinks it is a pretty good city but not much different than Sheridan, so he continues on to Chicago. In Chicago, he gets off the bus and marvels at the city. It is more than he had imagined. He walks around for a while and sees a bar that reminds him of the bars in Sheridan. He walks in and feels at home and buys a beer. But, it is early in the day, and he is alone so he sits and wishes he had someone to talk to. Soon, an attractive woman comes in and sits down. He has watched TV and knows you should buy an attractive woman a drink if you want to talk to her. So, he has the bartender bring her a drink with his compliments. She nods in appreciation. He has watched TV and knows now he should go sit by her and talk to her. So, he does. As he starts the conversation, she warns him, "I think you should know before you spend money on me that I am a lesbian." "I don't really know what that is," he replies. "A lesbian," says the woman, "is a person who would rather kiss a woman than a man on the lips." The cowhand thinks for a minute and then calls to the bartender. "Barkeep," he says, "bring two more drinks for us lesbians."

Two Elderly Women

Two elderly women in a nursing home were interested in two elderly gentlemen, living in the same home. But, try as they might, they couldn't get the attention of the men. Then, one of the women had a brilliant idea. "Why don't we strip off our clothes, and streak past them in the TV room?" The second woman agreed that this might work. The very next day, they mustered up their courage, took off their clothes, and ran past the two men as fast as they could, giggling all the way. One man turned to the other and said, "Joe, was that Irma that just ran past us?" The other one said, "I think so, but what the heck was she wearing?" The first one said, "I don't know, but it sure needs ironing!"

The Golden Wedding Anniversary

A couple was celebrating their golden wedding anniversary. Their domestic tranquility had long been the talk of the town. A local newspaper reporter was inquiring as to the secret of their long and happy marriage. "Well, it dates back to our honeymoon," explained the lady. "We visited the Grand Canyon and took a trip down to the bottom of the canyon by pack mule. We hadn't gone too far when my husband's mule stumbled. My husband quietly said, 'That's once.' We proceeded a little farther when the mule stumbled again. Once more my husband quietly said, 'That's twice.' We hadn't gone a half-mile when the mule stumbled a third time. My husband took a pistol from his pocket and shot him. I started to protest over his treatment of the mule when he looked at me and quietly said, 'That's once'."

A Visit To The Sex Therapist

A couple, both age 67, went to a sex therapist's office. The doctor asked, "What can I do for you?" The man said, "Will you watch us have sexual intercourse?" The doctor looked puzzled, but agreed. When the couple finished, the doctor said, "There's nothing wrong with the way you have intercourse," and charged them $50. This happened several weeks in a row. The couple would make an appointment, have intercourse with no problems, pay the doctor, then leave. Finally the doctor asked, "Just exactly what are you trying to find out?" The old man said, "We're not trying to find out anything. She's married and we can't go to her house. I'm married and we can't go to my house. The Holiday Inn charges $90. The Hilton charges $108. We do it here for $50, and I get $43 back from Medicare."

The Sheerest Lingerie

A husband wants to buy his wife the sheerest lingerie he can find at Frederick's of Hollywood. "This is $200," says the saleswoman, showing him an item. "I want one that's more sheer," says he. "This one is $350." "Sheerer than that." "This is the sheerest we have. It's $500." "I'll take it!" he replies. The man goes home to his wife and shows it to her, saying, "Go put this on and come down to model it for me." She goes upstairs, opens the box and thinks, "This thing is so see-through that the old coot won't even notice if I'm wearing it or not. I can take it back for a refund and he won't know the difference." So, she comes out wearing nothing at all and strikes a pose at the top of the stairs. "So, how do you like it?" she asks. He looks at her a moment and says, "Well, you'd think for $500 they'd iron the thing."

<u>Animals</u>

<u>Doggie Style</u>

Two guys were car pooling home from work one day. Traffic was crawling along and they were both a bit bored. The driver was looking around and suddenly pointed at two dogs having sex in someone's front lawn. "Look," he shouted, "what are those dogs doing? Fighting?" The passenger, being a man of the world, replied, "They're having sex. Don't tell me that you have never had sex doggie style before." The driver, a bit embarrassed, admitted that he never had. His passenger said, "You have to try it. It's pretty cool. Here's what you do. Tonight when you get home, fix your wife a margarita and then suggest that you want to try this new sexual position." The driver thought a bit then decided he would give it a try. The next morning, the two commuters were back in the car and the passenger asked, "Well, how did it go?" The driver replied, "It was great. But, it took me SIX margaritas just to get my wife naked in the front yard!"

<u>The Buzzing Fly</u>

There was a fly buzzing around a barn one day when he happened on a pile of fresh cow manure. Due to the fact that it had been hours since his last meal, he flew down and began to eat. He ate and ate and ate. Finally, he decided he had eaten enough and tried to fly away. But, he had eaten too much though, and couldn't get off the ground. As he looked around wondering what to do, he spotted a pitchfork leaning up against the wall. He climbed to the top of the handle and jumped off, thinking that once he got airborne, he would be able to take flight. Unfortunately, he was wrong and dropped like a rock, splatting when he hit the ground. Dead!!
The moral to the story is: Never fly off the handle when you know you're full of crap.

<u>A Frog Goes Into A Bank</u>

A frog goes into a bank, and hops up to the loan officer. The frog says, "Hi, what's your name?" The loan officer says, "My name is John Paddywack. Can I help you?" The frog says, "Yeah, I'd like to borrow some money." The loan officer finds this a little odd, but gets out a form. He says, "Okay, what's your name?" The frog says, "Kermit Jagger." The loan officer says, "Really? Any relation to Mick Jagger?" The frog says, "Yeah, he's my dad." The loan officer says, "Okay. Ummm...do you have any collateral?" The frog hands the loan officer a pink ceramic elephant and says, "Will this do?" The loan officer says, "Hmmm...I'm not sure. Let me go check with the bank manager." The frog says, "Oh, tell him I said hi. He knows me." The loan officer goes back to the manager and says, "Excuse me, but there's this frog out there named Kermit Jagger who wants to borrow some money. All he has for collateral is this pink elephant thing, I'm not even sure what it is." The manager says, "It's a nick-nack, Paddywack. Give the frog a loan. His old man's a Rolling Stone."

7

Cow Buying, Car Dealer Style!

A farmer had been taken several times by the local car dealer. One day, the car dealer informed the farmer that he was coming over to purchase a cow. The farmer priced his unit as follows:

Basic cow	499.95
Shipping and handling	35.75
Extra stomach	79.25
Two-tone exterior	142.10
Produce storage compartment	126.50
Heavy duty straw chopper	189.60
Four spigot/high output drain system	149.20
Automatic fly swatter	88.50
Genuine cowhide upholstery	179.90
Deluxe dual horns	59.25
Automatic fertilizer attachment	339.40
4 x 4 traction drive assembly	884.16
Pre-delivery wash and comb	69.80

FARMERS SUGGESTED LIST PRICE: 2843.36
Additional dealer adjustments: 300.00

TOTAL LIST PRICE (Including options): $3143.36

The Gorilla Cage

It's a beautiful warm Spring day and a man and his wife are at the zoo. She's wearing a cute, loose-fitting, pink spring dress, sleeveless with straps. As they walk through the ape exhibit and pass in front of a very large gorilla, the gorilla goes ape. He jumps up on the bars, holding on with one hand (and 2 feet), grunting and pounding his chest with the free hand. He is obviously excited at the pretty lady in the wavy dress. The husband, noticing the excitement, suggests that his wife tease the poor fellow. The husband suggests she pucker her lips, wiggle her bottom, and play along. She does and the gorilla gets even more excited, making noises that would wake the dead. Then, the husband suggests that she let one of her straps fall, she does, and the gorilla is just about to tear the bars down. "Now try lifting your dress up your thighs," the husband suggests, "it will drive the gorilla absolutely crazy." Then, quickly the husband grabs his wife by the hair, rips open the door to the cage, flings her in with the gorilla and says, "Now, tell HIM you have a headache."

How To Give Your Cat A Pill

1. Grasp cat firmly in your arms. Cradle its head on your elbow, just as if you were giving a baby a bottle. Coo confidently, "That's a nice kitty." Drop pill into its mouth.

2. Retrieve cat from top of lamp and pill from under sofa.

3. Follow same procedure as in #1, but hold cat's front paws down with left hand and back paws down with elbow of right arm. Poke pill into its mouth with right forefinger.

4. Get cat from under bed. Get new pill from bottle. (Resist impulse to get new cat.)

5. Again proceed as in #1, except when you have cat firmly cradled in bottle-feeding position, sit down on edge of chair, fold your torso over cat, bring your right hand over your left elbow, open cat's mouth by lifting the upper jaw and pop the pill in quickly. Since your head is down by your knees, you won't be able to see what you're doing. (That's just as well.)

6. Leave cat hanging on drapes. Leave pill in your hair.
7. If you're a woman, have a good cry. If you're a man, have a good cry.
8. Now pull yourself together. Who's the boss here anyway? Retrieve cat and pill. Assuming position #1, say sternly, "Who's the boss here, anyway?" Open cat's mouth, take pill and…..Oooops!

9. This isn't working, is it? Collapse and think. Aha! Those flashing claws are causing the chaos.

10. Crawl to the linen closet. Drag back large beach towel. Spread towel on floor.
11. Retrieve cat from kitchen counter and pill from potted plant.
12. Spread cat on towel near one end with its head over long edge.
13. Flatten cat's front and back legs over its stomach. (Resist impulse to flatten cat.)
14. Roll cat in towel. Work fast; time and tabbies wait for no man or woman.

15. Resume position #1. Rotate your left hand to cat's head. Press its mouth at the jaw hinges like opening the petals of a snapdragon.

16. Drop pill into cat's mouth and poke gently. Voila! It's done.
17. Vacuum up loose fur (cat's). Apply bandages to wounds (yours).
18. Take two aspirins and lie down.
19. Retrieve pill that cat hacked-up while you were lying down.

How Many Dogs Does It Take To Put In A Light Bulb?
(These are the answers from dogs when they were asked.)

Golden Retriever: The sun is shining, the day is young, we've got our whole lives ahead of us, and you're inside worrying about a stupid burned-out light bulb?

Border Collie: Just one. And, I'll replace any wiring that's not up to code.

Dachshund: I can't reach the stupid lamp!

Toy Poodle: I'll just blow in the Border collie's ear and he'll do it. By the time he finishes rewiring the house, my nails will be dry.

Rottweiler: Go Ahead! Make me!

Shi-tzu: Puh-leeze, dah-ling. Let the servants do that.

Lab: Oh, me, me!!! Pleeeeeeze let me change the light bulb! Can I? Can I? Huh? Huh? Can I?

Malamute: Let the Border collie do it. You can feed me while he's busy.

Cocker Spaniel: Why change it? I can still pee on the carpet in the dark.

Doberman Pinscher: While it's dark, I'm going to sleep on the couch.

Mastiff: Mastiffs are NOT afraid of the dark.

Hound Dog: ZZZZZZZZZZZZZZZZZZZZZ

Chihuahua: Yo quiero Taco Bulb.

Irish Wolfhound: Can somebody else do it? I've got a hangover.

Pointer: I see it, there it is, right there...!

Greyhound: It isn't moving, so who cares?

Australian Shepherd: First, put all the light bulbs in a little circle...

Old English Sheep Dog: Light bulb? Light bulb? That thing I just ate was a light bulb?

Things We Can Learn From Dogs

Never pass up an opportunity to go for a joy ride.
Allow the experience of fresh air and the wind in your face to be pure ecstasy.
When loved ones come home, always run to greet them.
When it's in your best interest, practice obedience.
Let others know when they've invaded your territory.
Take naps and stretch before rising.
Romp, run, and play daily.
Eat with gusto and enthusiasm.
Be loyal.
Never pretend to be something you're not.
If what you want lies buried, dig until you find it.
When someone is having a bad day, be silent, sit close by, and nuzzle them gently.
Thrive on attention and let people touch you.
Avoid biting when a simple growl will do.
On hot days, drink lots of water and lie under a shady tree.
When you're happy, dance around and wag your entire body.
No matter how often you're scolded, don't buy into the guilt thing and pout; run
    right back and make friends.
Delight in the simple joy of a long walk.

Mike At The Zoo

A zoo had acquired a very rare species of female gorilla. Within a few weeks, the gorilla became very ornery and difficult to handle. Upon examination, the zoo veterinarian determined the problem; she was in heat. What to do? There was no male of this species available. While reflecting on their problem, the zoo administrators noticed Mike, an employee responsible for cleaning the animals' cages. Now Mike, it was rumored, possessed ample ability to satisfy any female, and he wasn't very bright. So, the zoo administrators thought they might have a solution. Perhaps they could entice Mike to satisfy the female gorilla. So he was approached with a proposition: would he be willing to "service" the gorilla for five hundred bucks? Mike replied that he might be interested, but would have to think the matter over. The following day, Mike announced that he would accept their offer, but only under three conditions: "First," he said, "I don't want to have to kiss her." "Second, I don't want anything to do with any offspring that may result from this union." The zoo administration quickly acceded to these conditions. But, what could be the third? "Well," said Mike, "I need a week to come up with the five hundred bucks."

The Moose Hunt

Two hunters went moose hunting every winter without success. Finally, they came up with a foolproof plan. They got a very authentic female moose costume and learned the mating call of a female moose. The plan was to hide in the costume, lure the bull, then come out of the costume and shoot the bull. They set themselves up on the edge of a clearing, donned their costume, and began to give the moose love call. Before long, their call was answered as a bull came crashing out of the forest and into the clearing. When the bull was close enough, the guy in front said, "Okay, let's get out and get him." After a moment that seemed like an eternity, the guy in the back shouted, "The zipper is stuck! What are we going to do!?" The guy in the front says, "Well, I'm going to start nibbling grass, but you'd better brace yourself."

The Camel

A Captain in the foreign legion was transferred to a desert outpost. On his orientation tour he noticed a very old, seedy looking camel tied out back of the enlisted men's barracks. He asked the Sergeant leading the tour, "What's the camel for?" The Sergeant replied, "Well sir, it's a long way from anywhere, and the men have natural sexual urges, so when they do, we have the camel." The Captain said, "Well, if it's good for morale, then I guess it's all right with me." After he had been at the fort for about 6 months, the Captain could not stand it anymore, so he told his Sergeant, "BRING IN THE CAMEL!!!" The Sarge shrugged his shoulders and led the camel into the Captain's quarters. The Captain got a foot stool and proceeded to have vigorous sex with the camel. As he stepped, satisfied, down from the stool and was buttoning his pants he asked the Sergeant, "Is that how the enlisted men do it?" The Sergeant replied, "Well sir, they usually just use it to ride into town."

The Stud Rooster

A farmer goes out one day and buys a brand new stud rooster for his chicken coop. The young rooster walks over to the old rooster and says, "Ok, old fellow, time to retire." The old rooster says, "You can't handle all these chickens... look at what it did to me!" The young rooster replies, "Now, don't give me a hassle about this. Time for the old to step aside and the young to take over, so take a hike." The old rooster says, "Aw, c'mon..... just let me have the two old hens over in the corner and I won't bother you." The young rooster says, "Scram! Beat it! You're washed up! I'm taking over." So, the old rooster says to the young rooster, "I'll tell you what, young fellow, I'll have a race with you around the farmhouse. Whoever wins the race gets domain of the chicken coop." The young rooster says, "You know I'm going to beat you, old man. So, just to be fair, I'm even going to give you a head start." They line up in back of the farm house, get a chicken to cluck "GO!" and the old rooster takes off running. About 15 seconds later the young rooster takes off after him. They round the front the farm house and the young rooster is only about 5 inches behind the old rooster and gaining fast. The farmer, sitting on the porch, looks up, sees what's going on, grabs his shotgun and BOOM! he blows the young rooster to bits. He sadly shakes his head and says, "Dammit, third gay rooster I bought this month!"

Stud Rooster 2

A farmer wanted to have his hens serviced, so he went to the market looking for a rooster. He was hoping he could get a special rooster--one that would service all of his many hens. When he told this to the market vendor, the vendor replied, "I have just the rooster for you. Henry here is the horniest rooster you will ever see!" So, the farmer took Henry back to the farm. Before setting him loose in the hen house, though, he gave Henry a little pep talk: "Henry," he said, "I'm counting on you to do your stuff." And, without a word, Henry strutted into the hen house. Henry was as fast as he was furious, mounting each hen like a thunderbolt. There was much squawking and many feathers flying, till Henry had finished having his way with each hen. But, Henry didn't stop there. Henry went into the barn and mounted all of the horses, one by one, and still at the same frantic pace. Then, he went to the pig house, where he did the same. The farmer, watching all of this with disbelief cried out, "Stop, Henry!! You'll kill yourself!" But, Henry continued, seeking out each farm animal in the same manner.

Well, the next morning, the farmer looked out and saw Henry lying there on the lawn. His legs were up in the air, his eyes rolled back, and his long tongue hanging out. A buzzard was already circling above Henry. The farmer walked up to Henry saying, "Oh, you poor thing. Look what you did. You've gone and killed yourself. I warned you little buddy." "Shhhhhhh," Henry whispered, "The buzzard's getting closer."

The Monkey

A guy walks into a bar with a monkey on his shoulder. The guy sits at the bar and starts talking to the bartender. While they're talking, the monkey walks over to the pool table, and eats one of the pool balls. The bartender says to the guy, "What the heck is wrong with your monkey? He just ate one of the pool balls!" The guy replies, "I can't help it. He eats anything and everything, and there doesn't seem to be a thing I can do to stop it." He takes the monkey, and leaves. A few days later, the guy shows up at the bar and again, he's got the monkey with him. This time, the monkey sits down at the bar, grabs a peanut from a dish, sticks it up his butt, then pulls it back out and eats it. The bartender says to the guy, "What the heck is he doing now?" "He still pretty much eats everything, but after the pool ball a few days ago, he checks to make sure it will fit before he eats something."

Here Come The Storks

Two storks are sitting in their nest: a father stork and baby stork. The baby stork is crying and crying and father stork is trying to calm him. "Don't worry, son. Your mother will come back. She's only bringing people babies and making them happy." The next night, it's father's turn to do the job. Mother and son are sitting in the nest, the baby stork is crying, and mother is saying, "Son, your father will be back as soon as possible, but now he's bringing joy to new mommies and daddies." A few days later, the stork's parents are desperate; their son is absent from the nest all night! Shortly before dawn, he returns and the parents ask him where he's been all night. The baby stork says, "Nowhere. Just scaring the hell out of college students!"

Jesus Is Watching You

A burglar broke into a house one night. He shone his flashlight around looking for valuables and when he picked up a CD player to place it in his sack a strange voice echoed from the dark, saying: "Jesus is watching you." He nearly jumped out of his skin, clicked his flashlight out, and froze. When he heard nothing more after a bit, he shook his head, promised himself a holiday after the next big score, then clicked the light back on and began searching for more valuables. Just as he pulled the stereo out so he could disconnect the wires, clear as a bell he heard, "Jesus is watching you." Freaked out, he shone his light around frantically, looking for the source of the voice. Finally, in the corner of the room, his flashlight beam came to rest on a parrot. "Did you say that?" he hissed at the parrot. "Yep," the parrot confessed, then squawked, "I'm just trying to warn you!" The burglar relaxed.... "Warn me, huh? Who the heck are you?" "Moses," replied the bird. "Moses!" the burglar laughed. "What kind of stupid people would name a parrot Moses?" The bird promptly answered, "Probably the same kind of people who would name a Rottweiler Jesus."

Crazy Glue Humor

Vermont native, Ronald Demuth, found himself in a difficult position yesterday. While touring the Eagle's Rock African Safari (Zoo) with a group of thespians from St. Petersburg, Russia, Demuth went overboard to show them one of America's many marvels. He demonstrated the effectiveness of "Crazy Glue" ... the hard way. Apparently, Demuth wanted to demonstrate just how good the adhesive was, so he put about 3 ounces of the adhesive in the palms of his hands, and jokingly placed them on the buttocks of a passing rhino. The rhino, a resident of the zoo for the past thirteen years, was not initially startled as it has been part of the petting exhibit since its arrival as a baby. However, once it became aware of its being involuntarily stuck to Demuth, it began to panic and ran around the petting area wildly making Demuth an unintended passenger. "Sally (the rhino) hasn't been feeling well lately. She had been very constipated. We had just given her a laxative and some depressants to relax her bowels, when Demuth played his juvenile prank," said James Douglass, caretaker.

During Sally's tirade two fences were destroyed, a shed wall was gored, and a number of small animals escaped. Also, during the stampede, three pygmy goats and one duck were stomped to death. As for Demuth, it took a team of medics and zoo caretakers over four hours to remove his hands from the rhino's buttocks. First, the animal had to be captured and calmed down. However, during this process the laxatives began to take hold and Demuth was repeatedly showered with over 30 gallons of rhino diarrhea. "It was tricky. We had to calm her down, while at the same time shield our faces from being pelted with rhino dung. I guess you could say that Demuth was into it up to his neck. Once she was under control, we had three people with shovels working to keep an air passage open for Mr. Demuth. We were able to tranquilize her and apply a solvent to remove his hands from her rear," said Douglass. "I don't think he'll be playing with Crazy Glue for a while." Meanwhile, the Russians, while obviously amused, also were impressed with the power of the adhesive. "I'm going to buy some for my children, but of course they can't take it to the zoo," commented Vladimir Zolnikov, leader of the troupe.

WashBiolSurv

According to the Knight-Ridder News Service, the inscription on the metal bands used by the U.S. Department of the Interior to tag migratory birds has been changed. The bands used to bear the address of the Washington Biological Survey, abbreviated: "Wash. Biol. Surv." until the agency received the following letter from an Arkansas camper:

"Dear Sirs: While camping last week I shot one of your birds. I think it was a crow. I followed the cooking instructions on the leg tag and want to tell you it was horrible." (wash-boil-serve)

As a result, the bands are now marked, "Fish and Wildlife Service."

Bear Alert

In light of the rising frequency of human/grizzly bear conflicts, the Department of Natural Resources is advising hikers, hunters and fishermen to take extra precautions and keep alert of bears while in the field. "We advise that outdoorsmen wear noisy little bells on their clothing so as not to startle bears that aren't expecting them. We also advise outdoorsmen to carry pepper spray with them in case of an encounter with a bear. It is also a good idea to watch out for fresh signs of bear activity. Outdoorsmen should recognize the difference between black bear and grizzly bear droppings. Black bear droppings are smaller and contain lots of berries and squirrel fur. Grizzly bear droppings smell like pepper and have little bells in it.

Two Men Bear Hunting

Two men went bear hunting. While one stayed in the cabin, the other went out looking for a bear. He soon found a huge bear, shot at it but only wounded it. When the enraged bear charged toward him, he dropped his rifle and started running for the cabin as fast as he could. He ran pretty fast but the bear was just a little faster and gained on him with every step. Just as he reached the open cabin door, he tripped and fell flat. Too close behind to stop, the bear tripped over him and went rolling into the cabin. The man jumped up, closed the cabin door and yelled to his friend inside, "You skin this one while I go and get another!"

Pet Alligator

A guy walks into a bar with a pet alligator by his side. He puts the alligator up on the bar. He turns to the astonished patrons. "I'll make you a deal. I'll open this alligator's mouth and place my genitals inside. Then, the gator will close his mouth for one minute. He'll then open his mouth and I'll remove my unit unscathed. In return for witnessing this spectacle, each of you will buy me a drink." The crowd murmured their approval. The man stood up on the bar, dropped his trousers, and placed his privates in the alligator's open mouth. The gator closed his mouth as the crowd gasped. After a minute, the man grabbed a beer bottle and rapped the alligator hard on the top of its head. The gator opened his mouth and the man removed his genitals, unscathed as promised. The crowd cheered and the first of his free drinks was delivered. The man stood up again and made another offer. "I'll pay anyone $100 who's willing to give it a try." A hush fell over the crowd. After a while, a hand went up in the back of the bar. A blonde woman timidly spoke up. "I'll try, but you have to promise not to hit me on the head with the beer bottle."

Cats And Dogs

What is a cat?

- Cats do what they want.
- They rarely listen to you.
- They are totally unpredictable.
- When you want to play, they want to be alone.
- When you want to be alone, they want to play.
- They expect you to cater to their every whim.
- They are moody.
- They leave hair everywhere.
- They drive you nuts and cost an arm and a leg.
Conclusion: They are tiny women in fur coats.

What is a dog?

- Dogs lie around all day, sprawled on the most comfortable piece of furniture in the house.
- They can hear a package of food opening half a block away, but they don't hear you when you are in the same room.
- They growl when they are not happy.
- When you want to play, they want to play.
- When you want to be alone, they want to play.
- They are great at begging.
- They will love you forever if you rub their tummies.
- They leave their toys everywhere.
- They do disgusting things with their mouths and then try to give you a kiss.
Conclusion: They are little men in fur coats

The Turkey and the Bull

A turkey was chatting with a bull:
"I would love to be able to get to the top of that tree," sighed the turkey, "but I haven't got the energy." "Well, why don't you nibble on some of my droppings?" replied the bull. "They're packed with nutrients." The turkey pecked at a lump of dung and found that it actually gave him enough strength to reach the first branch of the tree. The next day, after eating some more dung, he reached the second branch. Finally, after a fourth night, there he was proudly perched at the top of the tree. He was promptly spotted by a farmer, who shot the turkey out of the tree.
Moral of the story: Bullshit might get you to the top, but it won't keep you there.

Why Did The Chicken Cross The Road?

TEACHER:
Q: Why did the chicken cross the road?
A: To get to the other side.

PLATO:
Q: Why did the chicken cross the road?
A: For the greater good.

ARISTOTLE:
Q: Why did the chicken cross the road?
A: It is in the nature of chickens to cross roads.

KARL MARX:
Q: Why did the chicken cross the road?
A: It was a historical inevitability.

TIMOTHY LEARY:
Q: Why did the chicken cross the road?
A: Because that's the only trip the establishment would let it take.

SADDAM HUSSEIN:
Q: Why did the chicken cross the road?
A: This was an unprovoked act of rebellion and we were quite justified in dropping 50 tons of nerve gas on it.

RONALD REAGAN:
Q: Why did the chicken cross the road?
A: I forget.

LOUIS FARRAKHAN:
Q: Why did the chicken cross the road?
A: The road, you see, represents the black man. The chicken 'crossed' the black man in order to trample him and keep him down.

MARTIN LUTHER KING, JR.:
Q: Why did the chicken cross the road?
A: I envision a world where all chickens will be free to cross roads without having their motives called into question.

MOSES:
Q: Why did the chicken cross the road?
A: And, God came down from the Heavens, and he said unto the chicken, "Thou shalt cross the road." And, the chicken crossed the road, and there was much rejoicing.

FOX MULDER:
Q: Why did the chicken cross the road?
A: You saw it cross the road with your own eyes. How many more chickens have to cross the road for you to believe it?

RICHARD M. NIXON:
Q: Why did the chicken cross the road?
A: The chicken did not cross the road. I repeat, the chicken DID NOT cross the road.

MACHIAVELLI:
Q: Why did the chicken cross the road?
A: The point is that the chicken crossed the road. Who cares why? The end of crossing the road justifies whatever motive there was.

JERRY SEINFELD:
Q: Why did the chicken cross the road?
A: Why does anyone cross the road? I mean, why doesn't anyone ever think to ask, "What the heck was the chicken doing wandering around all over the place anyway?"

FREUD:
Q: Why did the chicken cross the road?
A: The fact that you are at all concerned that the chicken crossed the road reveals your underlying sexual insecurity.

BILL GATES:
Q: Why did the chicken cross the road?
A: I have just released the new Chicken Office 2000 (with integrated Internet Seed Explorer), which will not only cross roads, but will lay eggs, file your important documents, and balance your checkbook.

DARWIN:
Q: Why did the chicken cross the road?
A: Chickens, over great periods of time, have been naturally selected in such a way that they are genetically disposed to cross roads.

CAPTAIN JAMES T. KIRK:
Q: Why did the chicken cross the road?
A: To boldly go where no chicken has gone before.

EINSTEIN:
Q: Why did the chicken cross the road?
A: Whether the chicken crossed the road or the road moved beneath the chicken depends upon your frame of reference.

BUDDHA:
Q: Why did the chicken cross the road?
A: Asking the question denies your own chicken nature.

RALPH WALDO EMERSON:
Q: Why did the chicken cross the road?
A: The chicken did not cross the road - it transcended it.

ERNEST HEMINGWAY:
Q: Why did the chicken cross the road?
A: To die. In the rain.

COLONEL SANDERS:
Q: Why did the chicken cross the road?
A: I missed one?

BILL CLINTON:
Q: Why did the chicken cross the road?
A: I did not have a sexual relationship with that chicken.

BILL THE CAT:
Q: Why did the chicken cross the road?
A: Oop! Ack!

ANDERSEN CONSULTING:
Q: Why did the chicken cross the road?
A: Deregulation of the chicken's side of the road was threatening it's dominant market position. The chicken was faced with significant challenges to create and develop the competencies required for the newly competitive market. Anderson Consulting, in a partnering relationship with the client, helped the chicken by rethinking it's physical distribution strategy and implementation process. Using the Poultry Integration Model (PIM), Anderson helped the chicken use it's skills, methodologies, knowledge, capital and experiences to align the chickens people, processes and technology in support of it's overall strategy within a Program Management framework. Anderson Consulting convened a diverse cross-spectrum of road analysts and best chickens along with Anderson consultants with deep skills in the transportation industry to engage in a two day itinerary of meetings in order to leverage their personal knowledge capital, both tacit and explicit, and to enable them to synergize with each other in order to achieve the implicit goals of delivering and successfully architecting and implementing an enterprise-wide value framework across the continuum of poultry cross-median processes. The meeting was held in a park-like setting, enabling and creating an impactful environment which was strategically based, industry-focused, and built upon a consistent, clear and unified market message and aligned with the chicken's mission, vision and core values. This was conducive towards the creation of a total business integration solution.

DR. SEUSS:
Q: Why did the chicken cross the road?
A: Did the chicken cross the road?
   Did he cross it with a toad?
   Did he use a cattle goad?
   Yes the chicken crossed the road,
   but why he crossed it, no one told!

HAMLET:
Q: Why did the chicken cross the road?
A: Because 'tis better to suffer in the mind the slings and arrows of outrageous road maintenance than to take arms against a sea of oncoming vehicles...

OLIVER NORTH:
Q: Why did the chicken cross the road?
A: National Security was at stake.

O.J.:
Q: Why did the chicken cross the road?
A: It didn't. I was playing golf with that chicken at the time...Can I have my glove back now?

PYRRHO THE SKEPTIC:
Q: Why did the chicken cross the road?
A: What road?

EMILY DICKENSON:
Q: Why did the chicken cross the road?
A: Because it could not stop for death.

JOSEPH STALIN:
Q: Why did the chicken cross the road?
A: I don't care. Catch it. I need its eggs to make my omelet.

DOUGLAS ADAMS:
Q: Why did the chicken cross the road?
A: Forty-two.

FRIEDRICH NIETZCHE:
Q: Why did the chicken cross the road?
A: Because if you gaze too long across the Road, the Road gazes also across you.

J.R.R. TOLKEIN:

Q: Why did the chicken cross the road?

A: The chicken, sunlight coruscating off its radiant yellow-white coat of feathers, approached the dark, sullen asphalt road and scrutinized it intently with its obsidian-black eyes. Every detail of the thoroughfare leapt into blinding focus: the rough texture of the surface, over which countless tires had worked their relentless tread through the ages; the innumerable fragments of stone embedded within the lugubrious mass, perhaps quarried from the great pits where the Sons of Man labored not far from here; the dull black asphalt itself, exuding those waves of heat which distort the sight and bring weakness to the body; the other attributes of the great highway too numerous to give name. And, then it crossed it.

MALCOLM X:

Q: Why did the chicken cross the road?

A: Because it would get across that road by any means necessary.

GARY GYGAX:

Q: Why did the chicken cross the road?

A: Because I rolled a 64 on the "Chicken Random Behaviors" chart on page 497 of Volume 3 of the Chicken Master's Guide.

DARTH VADER:

Q: Why did the chicken cross the road?

A: Because it could not resist the power of the Dark Side.

INIGO:

Q: Why did the chicken cross the road?

A: Hello. My name is Inigo Montoya. You crossed my father's road. Prepare to die.

ARISTOTLE:

Q: Why did the chicken cross the road?

A: To actualize its potential.

ROSEANNE:

Q: Why did the chicken cross the road?

A: Urrrrrp. What chicken?

GEORGE BUSH:

Q: Why did the chicken cross the road?

A: To face a kinder, gentler thousand points of headlights.

JULIUS CAESAR:
Q: Why did the chicken cross the road?
A: To come, to see, to conquer.

OLIVER STONE:
Q: Why did the chicken cross the road?
A: The question is not, "Why did the chicken cross the road?" Rather, it is, "Who is crossing the road at the same time, whom we overlooked in our haste to observe the chicken crossing?

GENE RODDENBERRY:
Q: Why did the chicken cross the road?
A: To boldly go where no chicken has gone before.

ZENO OF ELEA:
Q: Why did the chicken cross the road?
A: To prove it could never reach the other side.

GRANDPA:
Q: Why did the chicken cross the road?
A: In my day, we didn't ask why the chicken crossed the road. If someone told us that the chicken crossed the road then that was good enough for us.

MACHIAVELLI:
Q: Why did the chicken cross the road?
A: So that its subjects will view it with admiration, as a chicken which has the daring and courage to boldly cross the road, but also with fear, for whom among them has the strength to contend with such a paragon of avian virtue? In such a manner is the princely chicken's dominion maintained.

JACQUES DERRIDA:
Q: Why did the chicken cross the road?
A: Any number of contending discourses may be discovered within the act of the chicken crossing the road, and each interpretation is equally valid as the authorial intent can never be discerned, because structuralism is DEAD, DAMMIT, DEAD!

THOMAS DE TORQUEMADA:
Q: Why did the chicken cross the road?
A: Give me ten minutes with the chicken and I'll find out.

B.F. SKINNER:
Q: Why did the chicken cross the road?
A: Because the external influences which had pervaded its sensorium from birth had caused it to develop in such a fashion that it would tend to cross roads, even while believing these actions to be of its own free will.

MARK TWAIN:
Q: Why did the chicken cross the road?
A: The news of its crossing has been greatly exaggerated.
CARL JUNG:
Q: Why did the chicken cross the road?
A: The confluence of events in the cultural gestalt necessitated that individual chickens cross roads at this historical juncture, and therefore synchronicitously brought such occurrences into being.

JEAN-PAUL SARTRE:
Q: Why did the chicken cross the road?
A: In order to act in good faith and be true to itself, the chicken found it necessary to cross the road.

SALVADOR DALI:
Q: Why did the chicken cross the road?
A: The Fish.

DARWIN:
Q: Why did the chicken cross the road?
A: It was the logical next step after coming down from the trees.

EMILY DICKENSON:
Q: Why did the chicken cross the road?
A: Because it could not stop for death.
EPICURUS:
Q: Why did the chicken cross the road?
A: For fun.

JOHANN FRIEDRICH VON GOETHE:
Q: Why did the chicken cross the road?
A: The eternal hen-principle made it do it.

WERNER HEISENBERG:
Q: Why did the chicken cross the road?
A: We are not sure which side of the road the chicken was on, but it was moving very fast.

DAVID HUME:
Q: Why did the chicken cross the road?
A: Out of custom and habit.

THE SPHINX:
Q: Why did the chicken cross the road?
A: You tell me.

HENRY DAVID THOREAU:
Q: Why did the chicken cross the road?
A: To live deliberately ... and suck all the marrow out of life.

MOLLY YARD:
Q: Why did the chicken cross the road?
A: It was a hen!

L. A. POLICE DEPARTMENT:
Q: Why did the chicken cross the road?
A: Give us five minutes with the chicken and we'll find out.

PAT BUCHANAN:
Q: Why did the chicken cross the road?
A: To steal a job from decent, hardworking Americans.

Blondes

The Blonde And The Coke Machine

A blonde on vacation in Las Vegas walks up to a Coke machine and puts in a coin. Out pops a coke. The blonde looks amazed and runs away to get some more coins. She returns and starts feeding the machine madly and of course the machine keeps feeding out drinks. Another person walks up behind the blonde and watches her antics for a few minutes before stopping and her and asking if someone else could have a go. The blonde spins around and shouts in her face, "Can't you see I'm winning."

Blonde Carpenters

Two blonde carpenters were working on a house. The one who was nailing down siding, would reach into her nail pouch, pull out a nail and either toss it over her shoulder or nail it in. The other blonde, figuring this was worth looking into, asked, "Why are you throwing those nails away?" The first blonde explained, "If I pull a nail out of my pouch and it's pointed toward *me* I throw it away 'cause it's defective. If it's pointed toward the *house*, then I nail it in!" The second blonde got completely ticked off and yelled, "You MORON!!! The nails pointed toward you aren't defective! They're for the OTHER side of the house!!"

A Lawyer And A Blonde

A lawyer and a blonde are sitting next to each other on a long flight from LA to NY. The lawyer leans over to her and asks if she would like to play a fun game. The blonde just wants to take a nap, so she politely declines and rolls over to the window to catch a few winks. The lawyer persists and explains that the game is really easy and a lot of fun. He explains, "I ask you a question, and if you don't know the answer, you pay me $5, and visa-versa." Again, she politely declines and tries to get some sleep. The lawyer, now somewhat agitated, says, "Okay, if you don't know the answer you pay me $5, and if I don't know the answer, I will pay you $50!" figuring that since she is a blonde that he will easily win the match. This catches the blonde's attention and, figuring that there will be no end to this torment unless she plays, agrees to the game.

The lawyer asks the first question. "What's the distance from the earth to the moon?" The blonde doesn't say a word, reaches in to her purse, pulls out a five-dollar bill and hands it to the lawyer. Now, it's the blonde's turn. She asks the lawyer, "What goes up a hill with three legs, and comes down with four?" The lawyer looks at her with a puzzled look. He takes out his laptop computer and searches all his references. He uses his satellite phone and searches the internet and the Library of Congress. Frustrated, he sends E-mails to all his coworkers and friends he knows. All to no avail. After over an hour, he wakes the blonde and hands her $50. The blonde politely takes the $50 and turns away to get back to sleep. The lawyer, who is more than a little miffed, wakes the blonde and asks, "Well, so what IS the answer!?" Without a word, the blonde reaches into her purse, hands the lawyer $5, and goes back to sleep.

A Skirt Too Tight For The Bus

In a crowded city at a crowded bus stop, a beautiful young blonde was waiting for the bus. She was decked out in a tight leather mini skirt with matching tight leather boots and jacket. As the bus rolled up and it became her turn to get on, she became aware that her skirt was too tight to allow her leg to come up to the height of the first step on the bus. Slightly embarrassed and with a quick smile to the bus driver, she reached behind her and unzipped her skirt a little thinking that this would give her enough slack to raise her leg. Again, she tried to make the step onto the bus only to discover she still couldn't! So, a little more embarrassed, she once again reached behind her and unzipped her skirt a little more and for a second time attempted the step. Once again, much to her chagrin she could not raise her leg because of the tight skirt. So, with a coy little smile to the driver, she again unzipped the offending skirt to give a little more slack and again was unable to make the step. About this time, the big Texan that was behind her in the line picked her up easily from the waist and placed her lightly on the step of the bus. Well, she went ballistic and turned on the would-be hero screeching at him, "How dare you touch my body!! I don't even know who you are!" At this the Texan drawled, "Well ma'am, normally I would agree with you but after you unzipped my fly three times, I kinda figured that we was friends."

Three Blondes Died

Three blondes died and are at the pearly gates of Heaven. St. Peter tells them that they can enter if they can answer one simple question. St. Peter asks the 1st blonde, "What is Easter?" The blonde replies, "Oh, that's easy. It's the holiday in November when everyone gets together and eats and are thankful..." "Wrong," replies St. Peter. He then asks the 2nd blonde, "What is Easter?" The 2nd blonde replies, "Easter is the holiday in December when we put up a nice tree, exchange presents, and celebrate the birth of Jesus." "Wrong," replies St. Peter in disgust. He looks at the 3rd blonde and says, "Well, do you know what Easter is?" The 3rd blonde confidently replies, "Easter is the Christian holiday that coincides with the celebration of Passover. Jesus and his disciples were eating at the Last Supper and Jesus was later deceived and turned over to the Romans. The Romans took Him to be crucified and He was stabbed in the side, made to wear a crown of thorns, and was hung on a cross with nails through His hands. He was buried in a nearby cave which was sealed off by a large boulder." St. Peter smiles broadly with delight. The 3rd blonde continues, "Every year the boulder is moved aside so that Jesus can come out and if He sees His shadow, there will be 6 more weeks of winter."

Blonde Jokes

1. What do you call an eternity?
   Four Blondes in four cars at a four way stop.

2. Why do Blondes have TGIF written on their shoes?
   Toes Go In First.

3. Three Blondes were driving to Disneyland. After being in the car for four hours
   they   finally saw a sign that said "Disneyland Left" so they turned around and
   went home.

4. What do SMART Blondes and UFO's have in common?
   You always hear about them but never see them.

5. What did the Blonde say when she opened the box of Cheerios?
   "Oh look, Daddy...Doughnut seeds."

6. Why did the Blonde stare at the can of frozen orange juice?
   Because it said concentrate.

Elmo Doll Factory

A very modest blonde woman applied for a job at the factory where they
made the "Tickle-Me-Elmo dolls." It was Friday and almost quitting time and
hurriedly the boss told her to report for work on Monday and then explained she
would be stationed on the assembly line just before the dolls were packed into boxes.
Monday they started up the line and within twenty minutes had to shut it down
because one worker couldn't keep up. The boss went down the line to find the
problem. The new employee was very busy trying to do her part but she had a bunch
of dolls waiting for her. Closer examination showed she was sewing little cloth bags
containing two walnuts in the appropriate place on the dolls. When the boss could
control his laughter he said, "Lady, I said to give each doll two test-tickles."

Gave It Up For Lent

On the first day of their Honeymoon, the very naive blond virgin bride
slipped into a sexy but sweet nightie and, with great anticipation, crawled into bed,
only to find that her new Christian husband had settled down on the couch. When
she asked him why he was apparently not going to make love to her, he replied,
"Because it's Lent." Almost in tears, she remarked, "Well, that is the most ridiculous
thing I have ever heard! To whom did you lend it, and for how long?"

Blonde With Two Red Ears

A blonde with two red ears went to her doctor. The doctor asked her what had happened to her ears and she answered, "I was ironing a shirt when the phone rang, but instead of picking up the phone, I accidentally picked up the iron and stuck it to my ear." "Oh, dear!" the doctor exclaimed in disbelief. "But what happened to your other ear?" "The son of a gun called back."

A Blonde Goes Ice-Fishing

A blonde wanted to go ice fishing. She'd seen many books on the subject, and finally, after getting all the necessary "tools" together, she made for the nearest frozen lake. After positioning her comfy footstool, she started to make a circular cut in the ice. Suddenly, from the sky, a voice boomed, "THERE ARE NO FISH UNDER THE ICE!" Startled, the blonde moved further down the ice, poured a Thermos of cappuccino, and began to cut yet another hole. Again, from the heavens, the voice bellowed, "THERE ARE NO FISH UNDER THE ICE!" The Blonde, now quite worried, moved way down to the opposite end of the ice, set up her stool, and tried again to cut her hole. The voice came once more, "THERE ARE NO FISH UNDER THE ICE!" She stopped, looked skyward, and said, "Is that you, Lord?" The voice replied, "NO, THIS IS THE MANAGER OF THE ICE RINK."

For The Ladies

<u>A Woman And Her Lover</u>

A woman is in bed with her lover who also happens to be her husband's best friend. They make love for hours, and afterwards, while they're just laying there, the phone rings. Since it is the woman's house, she picks up the receiver. Her lover looks over at her and listens, only hearing her side of the conversation...(She is speaking in a cheery voice) "Hello? Oh, hi. I'm so glad that you called. Really? That's wonderful. I am so happy for you. That sounds terrific. Great! Thanks. Okay. Bye bye." She hangs up the telephone and her lover asks, "Who was that?" "Oh" she replies, "That was my husband telling me all about the wonderful time he's having on his fishing trip with you."

<u>Male Development</u>

This explains everything ....

All babies start out with the same number of raw cells which, over nine months, develop into a complete female baby. The problem occurs when cells are instructed by the little chromosomes to make a male baby instead. Because there are only so many cells to go around, the cells necessary to develop a male's reproductive organs have to come from cells already assigned elsewhere in the female. Recent tests have shown that these cells are removed from the communications center of the brain, migrate lower in the body and develop into male sexual organs. If you visualize a normal brain to be similar to a full deck of cards, this means that males are born a few cards short, so to speak. And some of their cards are in their shorts.

This difference between the male and female brain manifests itself in various ways. Little girls will tend to play things like house or learn to read. Little boys, however, will tend to do things like placing a bucket over their heads and running into walls. Little girls will think about doing things before taking any action. Little boys will just punch or kick something and will look surprised if someone asks them why they just punched their little brother who was half asleep and looking the other way. This basic cognitive difference continues to grow until puberty, when the hormones kick into action and the trouble really begins.

After puberty, not only the size of the male and female brains differ, but the center of thought also differs. Women think with their heads. Male thoughts often originate lower in their bodies where their ex-brain cells reside. Of course, the size of this problem varies from man to man. In some men, only a small number of brain cells migrate and they are left with nearly full mental capacity but they tend to be rather dull, sexually speaking. Such men are known in medical terms as "Republicans." Other men suffer larger brain cell relocation. These men are medically referred to as "Democrats." A small number of men suffer massive brain cell migration to their groins. These men are usually referred to as....."Mr. President."

Great Quotes By Great Ladies

I'm not offended by all the dumb blonde jokes because I know I'm not dumb...and I also know that I'm not blonde.
- Dolly Parton

You see a lot of smart guys with dumb women, but you hardly ever see a smart woman with a dumb guy.
- Erica Jong

I want to have children, but my friends scare me. One of my friends told me she was in labor for 36 hours. I don't even want to do anything that feels GOOD for 36 hours.
- Rita Rudner

I figure that if the children are alive when I get home, I've done my job.
- Roseanne

My husband and I are either going to buy a dog or have a child. We can't decide to ruin our carpet or ruin our lives.
- Rita Rudner

I was on a date recently, and the guy took me horseback riding. That was kind of fun, until we ran out of quarters.
- Susie Loucks

He tricked me into marrying him. He told me he was pregnant.
- Carol Leifer

I've been on so many blind dates, I should get a free dog.
- Wendy Liebman

Never lend your car to anyone to whom you have given birth to.
- Erma Bombeck

If high heels were so wonderful, men would be wearing them.
- Sue Grafton

I'm not going to vacuum 'til Sears makes one you can ride on.
- Roseanne

I would love to speak a foreign language, but I can't. So I grew hair under my arms instead.
- Sue Kolinsky

"When women are depressed they either eat or go shopping. Men invade another country."
- Elayne Boosler

"I base most of my fashion taste on what doesn't itch."
- Gilda Radner

"Behind every successful man is a surprised woman."
- Maryon Pearson

"In politics, if you want anything said, ask a man; if you want anything done, ask a woman."
- Margaret Thatcher

"I have yet to hear a man ask for advice on how to combine marriage and a career."
- Gloria Steinem

"I never married because there was no need. I have three pets at home which answer the same purpose as a husband. I have a dog which growls every morning, a parrot which swears all afternoon and a cat that comes home late at night."
- Marie Corelli

"I am a marvelous housekeeper. Every time I leave a man I keep his house."
- Zsa Zsa Gabor

Sara Lee

A husband is at home watching a football game when his wife interrupts, "Honey, could you fix the light in the hallway? It's been flickering for weeks now." He looks at her and says angrily, "Fix the light? Now? Does it look like I have G.E. printed on my forehead? I don't think so." "Well then, could you fix the fridge door? It won't close right." To which he replied, "Fix the fridge door? Does it look like I have Westinghouse written on my forehead? I don't think so." "Fine," she says. "Then, could you at least fix the steps to the front door? They're about to break." I'm not a damn carpenter and I don't want to fix the steps," he says. Does it look like I have Ace Hardware written on my forehead I don't think so. I've had enough of you. I'm going to the bar to finish watching the game." So, he goes to the bar, watches the game and drinks for a couple of hours. He starts to feel guilty about how he treated his wife, and decides to go home and help out. As he walks into the house, he notices the steps are already fixed. As he enters the house, he sees the hall light is working. As he goes to get another beer, he notices the fridge door is fixed. "Honey how'd this all get fixed?" She said, "Well, when you left I sat outside and cried. Just then, a nice young man asked me what was wrong, and I told him. He offered to do all the repairs and all I had to do was either go to bed with him or bake him a cake. He said, "So, what kind of cake did you bake him?" She replied, "Hello.................do you see Sara Lee written on my forehead?"

J.D. Heskin

Men Are Like...

Men are like a fine wine:
They all start out like grapes, and it's our job to stomp on them and keep them in the dark until they mature into something you'd want to have dinner with.

Men are like vacations:
They never seem to last long enough

Men are like computers:
Hard to figure out and never have enough memory.

Men are like coolers:
Load them with beer, and you can take them anywhere.

Men are like coffee:
The best ones are rich, warm, and can keep you up all night long.

Men are like horoscopes:
They always tell you what to do, and they're usually wrong.

Men are like plungers:
They spend most of their time in a hardware store or the bathroom.

Men are like snowstorms:
You never know when they're coming, how many inches you'll get, or how long it will last.

Men are like parking spots:
The good ones are taken, and the rest are too small or handicapped.

Men are like.....Placemats.
They only show up when there's food on the table.

Men are like.....Mascara.
They usually run at the first sign of emotion.

Men are like.....Bike helmets.
Handy in an emergency, but otherwise they just look silly.

Men are like.....Government bonds.
They take too long to mature.

Men are like.....Copiers.
You need them for reproduction, but that's about it.

Men are like.....Lava lamps.
Fun to look at but not all that bright.

Men are like.....Bank accounts.
Without a lot of money, they don't generate much interest.

Men are like.....High heels.
They're easy to walk on once you get the hang of it.

Preparing For Your Mammogram

Many women are afraid of their first mammogram, but there is no need to worry. By taking a few minutes each day for a week preceding the exam and doing the following practice exercises, you will be totally prepared for the test. And, best of all, you can do these simple practice exercises right in your own home!

Exercise 1: Open your refrigerator door and insert one breast between the door and the main box. Have one of your strongest friends slam the door shut as hard as possible and lean on the door for good measure. Hold that position for five seconds. Repeat again in case the first time wasn't effective enough.

Exercise 2: Visit your garage at 3am when the temperature of the cement floor is just perfect. Take off all of your clothes and lie comfortably on the floor with one breast wedged under the rear tire of the car. Ask a friend to slowly back the car up until your breast is sufficiently flattened and chilled. Turn over and repeat for the other breast.

Exercise 3: Freeze two metal bookends overnight. Strip to the waist. Invite a stranger into the room. Press the bookends against one of your breasts. Smash the bookends together as hard as you can. Set an appointment with the stranger to meet next year and do it again!

Congratulations!! Now you are properly prepared for your mammogram.

Why It's Good To Be A Woman

We got off the Titanic first.

We can scare male bosses with mysterious gynecological disorder excuses.

Our boy friend's clothes make us look elfin and gorgeous. Guys look like complete idiots in ours.

We can be groupies. But, male groupies are stalkers.

We've never lusted after a cartoon character or the central figure in a computer game.

Taxis stop for us.

Men die earlier, so we get to cash in on the life insurance.

We don't look like a frog in a blender when dancing.

We can hug our friends without wondering if they think we're gay.

We can hug our friends without wondering if WE'RE gay.

We know The Truth about whether size matters.

It's possible to live our whole lives without ever taking a group shower.

No fashion faux pas we make could rival The Speedo.

We don't have to fart to amuse ourselves.

If we forget to shave, no one has to know.

We can congratulate our teammate without ever touching her ass.

If we have a zit, we know how to conceal it.

We never have to reach down every-so-often to make sure our privates are still there.

If we're dumb, some people will find it cute.

We don't have to memorize Caddyshack or Fletch to fit in.

We have the ability to dress ourselves.

We can talk to people of the opposite sex without having to picture them naked.

If we marry someone 20 years younger, we're aware that we look like an idiot.

Our friends won't think we're weird if we ask whether there's spinach in our teeth.

There are times when chocolate really can solve all your problems.

Gay waiters don't make us uncomfortable.

We'll never regret piercing our ears.

We can fully assess a person just by looking at their shoes.

We know which glass was ours by the lipstick mark.

Why Nagging A Man Doesn't Work

What a woman **says**:
"This place is a mess! C'mon,
You and I need to clean up.
Your stuff is lying on the floor
and you'll have no clothes to wear
if we don't do laundry right now!"

What a man **hears**:
blah, blah, blah, blah, C'MON
blah, blah, blah, YOU AND I
blah, blah ON THE FLOOR
blah, blah, blah, NO CLOTHES,
blah blah, blah, blah, blah, RIGHT NOW!

J.D. Heskin

If Women Ran The World...

A man would no longer be considered a "good catch" simply because he is breathing.

Medical research money would be spent on developing new birth control methods for men.

Women with cold hands would give men prostate exams.

Baby-sitting, doing dishes and making beds would be considered "Macho."

The hem of men's pants would go up or down depending on the economy.

Men would be forced to purchase overpriced clothes every season.

Minnie Mouse would get equal billing with Mickey.

Fewer women would be dieting because the ideal weight standard would increase by 40 pounds.

Overweight men would be encouraged to wear girdles.

PMS would be a legitimate defense in court.

Men would come with papers showing their true identity, marital and employment status, if they live with their mother, and whether they have had their shots.

Shopping would be considered an aerobic activity.

Men would get great reputations for sleeping around.

"Ms Magazine" would have an annual swimsuit issue featuring scantily clad male models.

Men who designed women's shoes would be forced to wear them.

Men would not be allowed to eat gas-producing foods within two hours of bedtime.

Men would be as attentive AFTER marriage as they were before. Men would be secretaries for female bosses, working twice as hard for none of the credit.

Little girls would read "Snow White and the Seven Hunks."

Men would earn 70 cents for every dollar women make.

Men would bring drinks, chips and dip to women watching soap operas.

Men would HAVE to get Playboy for the articles, because there would be no pictures.

Men would learn phrases like: I'm sorry, I love you, you're beautiful. Of course, you don't look fat in that outfit. Go to sleep-I'll take care of the baby, etc.

Men would be judged entirely by their looks, women by their accomplishments.

Men would sit around and wonder what WE are thinking.

Men would pay as much attention to their women as their cars.

All toilet seats would be nailed down.

Men would work on relationships as much as they work on their careers.

TV news segments on sports would never run longer than one minute.

All men would be forced to spend one month in a PMS simulator.

Men would have their wedding rings permanently attached so they can't pretend to be single.

During mid-life crisis, men would get hot-flashes and women would date 19 year old boys.

Overweight men would have their weight brought to their attention constantly.

After a baby is born, men would take a six-week paternity leave to wait on their wives hand and foot.

For basic training, soldiers would have to take care of a two-year old for six weeks.

A female employee would be noticed for her work performance, not her bra size.

Singles bars would have metal detectors to weed out men hiding wedding rings in their pockets.

The New Over 40 Barbie

1. **Bifocals Barbie**. Comes with her own set of blended-lens fashion frames in six wild colors (half-frames too!), neck chain and large-print editions of Vogue and Martha Stewart Living.

2. **Hot Flash Barbie**. Press Barbie's bellybutton and watch her face turn beet red while tiny drops of perspiration appear on her forehead! With hand-held fan and tiny tissues.

3. **Facial Hair Barbie**. As Barbie's hormone levels shift, see her whiskers grow! Available with teensy tweezers and magnifying mirror.

4. **Cook's Arms Barbie**. Hide Barbie's droopy triceps with these new, roomier-sleeved gowns. Good news on the tummy front, too: muu-muus are back! Cellulite cream and loofah sponge optional.

5. **Bunion Barbie**. Years of disco dancing in stiletto heels have definitely taken their toll on Barbie's dainty arched feet. Soothe her sores with this pumice stone and plasters, then slip on soft terry mules. Colors: pink, rose, blush.

6. **No More Wrinkles Barbie**. Erase those pesky crow's-feet and lip lines with a tube of Skin Sparkle-Spackle, from Barbie's own line of exclusive age-blasting cosmetics.

7. **Soccer Mom Barbie**. All that experience as a cheerleader is really paying off as Barbie dusts off her old high school megaphone to root for Babs and Ken Jr.. With minivan in robin's egg blue or white, and cooler filled with doughnut holes and fruit punch.

8. **Midlife Crisis Barbie**. It's time to ditch Ken. Barbie needs a change, and Bruce (her personal trainer) is just what the doctor ordered, along with Prozac. They're hopping in her new red Miata and heading for the Napa Valley to open a B&B. Comes with real tape of "Breaking Up Is Hard to Do."

9. **Single Mother Barbie**. There's not much time for primping anymore! Ken's shacked up with the Swedish au pair in the Dream House and Barbie's across town with Babs and Ken Jr. in a fourth floor walk-up. Barbie's selling off her old gowns and accessories to raise rent money. Complete garage sale kit included.

10. **Recovery Barbie**. Too many parties have finally caught up with the ultimate party girl. Now she does 12 steps instead of dance steps! Clean and sober, she's going to meetings religiously. Comes with little copy of The Big Book and six-pack of Diet Coke.

Ladies Night Club

So, the other day, my friends and I went to this "Ladies Night Club. "One of the girls wanted to impress us, so she pulls out a $10 bill. The "dancer" came over to us, and my friend licked the $10 and put it on his butt cheek. Not to be outdone, another friend pulls out a $20 bill. She calls the guy back over, licks the $20 bill and puts it on his other butt cheek. Still attempting to impress the rest of us, my other friend pulls out a $50 bill. She calls the guy back over again, licks the $50 bill and again puts it on one of his butt cheeks. Now the attention is focused on me. What could I do to top that? I got out my wallet, thought for a minute and then the financial analyst in me took over. I got out my ATM card, swiped it down the crack of his ass, grabbed the $80 bucks and went home.

Labor Pain

A married couple went to the hospital together to have their baby delivered. Upon their arrival, the doctor said he had invented a new device that would transfer a portion of the mother's labor pains to the father. He asked if they were willing to try it out. They were both very much in favor of it. The doctor set the knob to 10% for starters, explaining that even 10% was probably more pain than the father had ever experienced before. As the labor progressed, the husband felt fine, so he asked the doctor to bump it up a notch. The doctor adjusted the machine to 20% pain transfer. The husband still felt fine. The doctor checked the husband's vital signs and was amazed at how well he was doing. At this, they decided to try 50%. The husband continued to feel quite well. Since it was obviously helping the wife considerably, he encouraged the doctor to transfer ALL the pain to him. The wife delivered a healthy baby boy with virtually no pain. She and her husband were ecstatic. When they got home, however, the mailman was lying dead on their porch.

Just Like A Man!

Brenda, pregnant with her first child, was paying a visit to her obstetrician's office. When the exam was over, she shyly began, "My husband wants me to ask you..." "I know, I know," the doctor said, placing a reassuring hand on her shoulder, "I get asked this all the time. Sex is fine until late in the pregnancy." "No, that's not it at all," Brenda confessed. "He wants to know if I can still mow the lawn."

What's With The Remote?

"Cash, check or charge?" the cashier asked after folding items the woman wished to purchase. As the woman fumbled for her wallet, the cashier noticed a remote control for a television set in her purse. "Do you always carry your TV remote?" the cashier asked. "No," she replied, "but my husband refused to come shopping with me, so I figured this was the most evil thing I could do to him."

Jokes Women Love

Q: How many honest, intelligent, caring men in the world does it take to do the dishes?
A: Both of them.

Q: What do men and sperm have in common?
A: They both have a one-in-a-million chance of becoming a human being

Q: How are men and parking spots alike?
A: Good ones are always taken. Free ones are mostly handicapped or extremely small.

Q: How does a man show that he is planning for the future?
A: He buys two cases of beer.

Q: What is the difference between men and government bonds?
A: The bonds mature.

Q: Why are blonde jokes so short?
A: So men can remember them.

Q: How many men does it take to change a roll of toilet paper?
A: We don't know; it has never happened.

Q: Why is it difficult to find men who are sensitive, caring good-looking?
A: They all already have boyfriends.

Q: What do you call a woman who knows where her husband is at night?
A: A Widow.

Q: How did Pinocchio find out he was made of wood?
A: His hand caught fire.

Q: How do you get a man to do sit-ups?
A: Put the remote control between his toes.

Q: What did God say after creating Adam?
A: I must be able to do better than that.

Q: What did God say after creating Eve?
A: "Practice makes perfect."

Q: What is the one thing that all men at singles bars have in common?
A: They are married.

"Just Her Size" (Men Are From Sears, Women Are From Nordstrom)

I believe that, in general, women are saner than men. For example, If you see people who have paid good money to stand in an outdoor stadium on a freezing December day wearing nothing on the upper halves of their bodies except paint, those people will be male. Without males, there would be no such sport as professional lawn mower racing. Also, there would be a 100% decline in the annual number of deaths related to efforts to shoot beer cans off of heads. Also, if women were in charge of all the world's nations, there would be, I sincerely believe this, virtually no military conflicts, and if there were a military conflict, everybody involved would feel just awful and there would soon be a high-level exchange of thoughtful notes written on greeting cards with flowers on the front, followed by a Peace Luncheon (which would be salads, with the dressing on the side).

So, I sincerely believe that women are wiser than men, with the exception of one key area, and that area is: clothing sizes. In this particular area, women are insane. When a man shops for clothes, his primary objective is to purchase clothes that fit on his particular body. A man will try on a pair of pants, and if those pants are too small, he'll try on a larger pair, and when he finds a pair that fits, he buys them. Most men do not spend a lot of time fretting about the size of their pants. Many men wear jeans with the size printed right on the back label, so that if you're standing behind a man in a supermarket line, you can read his waist and inseam size. A man could have, say, a 52-inch waist and a 30-inch inseam, and his label will proudly display this information, which is basically the same thing as having a sign that says, "Howdy! My butt is the size of a Federal Express truck!" The situation is very different with women.

When a woman shops for clothes, her primary objective is NOT to find clothes that fit her particular body. She would like for that to be the case, but her primary objective is to purchase clothes that are the size she wore when she was 19 years old. This will be some arbitrary number such as "5" or "7." Don't ask me "5" or "7" of what; that question has baffled scientists for centuries. All I know is that if a woman was a size 5 at age 19, she wants to be a size 5 now, and if a size 5 outfit does not fit her, she will not move on to a larger size: She can't! Her size is 5! So, she will keep trying on size 5 items, and unless they start fitting her, she will become extremely unhappy.

She may take this unhappiness out on her husband, who is waiting patiently in the mall, perhaps browsing in the Sharper Image store, trying to think of how he could justify purchasing a pair of night-vision binoculars. "Hi!" he'll say, when his wife finds him. "You know how sometimes the electricity goes out at night and..." "Am I fat?" she'll ask, cutting him off. This is a very bad situation for the man, because if he answers "yes," she'll be angry because he's saying that she's fat, and if he answers "no," she'll be angry because HE'S OBVIOUSLY LYING BECAUSE NONE OF THE SIZE 5's FIT HER. There is no escape for the husband. I think a lot of unexplained disappearances occur because guys in malls see their wives unsuccessfully trying on outfits, and they realize their lives will be easier if, before their wives come out and demand to know whether they're fat, the guys just run off and join a UFO cult. The other day, my wife, Michelle, was in a terrific mood, and you know why? Because she had successfully put on a size 6 outfit. She said this made her feel wonderful. She said, and this is a direct quote: "I wouldn't care if these pants were this big (here she held her arms far apart) as long as they have a '6' on them."

Here's how you could get rich: Start a women's clothing store called "SIZE 2," in which all garments, including those that were originally intended to be restaurant awnings, had labels with the words, "SIZE 2." I bet you'd sell clothes like crazy. You'd probably get rich, and you could retire, maybe take up some philanthropic activity to benefit humanity. I'm thinking here of professional lawn mower racing.

Feminist Fairy Tale

Once upon a time, a beautiful, independent, self assured princess happened upon a frog in a pond. The frog said to the princess, "I was once a handsome prince until an evil witch put a spell on me. One kiss from you and I will turn back into a prince and then we can marry, move into the castle with my mom, and you can prepare my meals, clean my clothes, bear my children and be forever happy doing so." That night, while the princess dined on frogs legs, she laughed to herself and thought, "I don't frickin' think so."

For The Men

J.D. Heskin

What Men Know

Men know that Mother Nature's best aphrodisiac is still a naked woman.

Men know that PMS is Mother Nature's way of telling you to get out of the house.

Men know that if she looks like her mother, run.

Men know that there are at least three sides to every story: his, hers, and the truth.

Men know never to run away from a fight that you know you can win.

Men know that cats are evil and cannot be trusted.

Men know how to change the toilet paper, but to do so would ruin the game.

Men know exactly how much gas is left in the tank and how far that gas will get them.

Men know that dating women are often psychic, usually knowing how a date will end even before it starts.

Men know that from time to time, it is absolutely necessary to adjust oneself.

Men know that a woman will wear a low-cut dress and expect the man to stare at her cleavage.

Men also know that the woman will get ticked off when they do, for reasons not totally clear to them.

Men know that the reason men don't like cats is because they don't know how to cook them.

Men know that there is no such thing as a sure thing, unless her name is Bambi.

Men know that it's never a good idea to tell your father-in-law how good his daughter is in bed.

Men know that men are from here, and women are from way the hell over there.

Who Talks More?

A husband was trying to show his wife that women talk much more than men. To prove his point, he showed her a scholarly study that showed men, on average, use about 1,500 words per day, while women use at least 3,000. His wife pondered this for a moment and said, "Women use twice as many words as men, because they have to repeat everything they say." "What?" the husband answered.

Quiz For The Men

You should make love to a woman for the first time only after you've both shared:
a) your views about what you expect from a sexual relationship
b) your blood-test results
c) five tequila slammers

You time your orgasm so that:
a) your partner climaxes first
b) you both climax simultaneously
c) you don't miss SportsCenter

Passionate, spontaneous sex on the kitchen floor is:
a) healthy, creative love-play
b) not the sort of thing your wife/girlfriend would ever agree to
c) not the sort of thing your wife/girlfriend need ever find out about

Spending the whole night cuddling a woman you've just had sex with is:
a) the best part of the experience
b) the second best part of the experience
c) $100 extra

Your girlfriend says she's gained five pounds in weight in the last month.
You tell her that it is:
a) no concern of yours
b) not a problem, she can join your gym
c) a conservative estimate

You think today's sensitive, caring man is:
a) a myth
b) an oxymoron
c) a moron

Foreplay is to sex as:
a) appetizer is to entree
b) primer is to paint
c) a line is to an amusement park ride

Which of the following are you most likely to find yourself saying at the end of a relationship?
a) "I hope we can still be friends."
b) "I'm not in right now, please leave a message at the beep."
c) "Welcome to Dumpsville, population, YOU."

If you answered "a" more than 5 times, check your pants to make sure you really are a man. If you answered "b" more than 5 times, check into therapy, you're still a little confused. If you answered "c" more than 5 times, "You da MAN!"

If Men Really Ruled The World
(from November 1998 issue of Maxim Magazine)

Any fake phone number a girl gave you would automatically forward your call to her real number.

Nodding and looking at your watch would be deemed an acceptable response to "I love you."

Hallmark would make "Sorry, what was your name again?" cards.

When your girlfriend really needed to talk to you during the game, she'd appear in a little box in the corner of the screen during a time-out.

Breaking up would be a lot easier. A smack to the ass and a "Nice hustle, you'll get 'em next time" would pretty much do it.

Birth control would come in ale or lager.

You'd be expected to fill your resume with gag names of people you'd worked for, like "Heywood J' Blowme."

Each year, your raise would be pegged to the fortunes of the NFL team of your choice.

The funniest guy in the office would get to be CEO.

"Sorry I'm late, but I got really wasted last night" would be an acceptable excuse for tardiness.

At the end of the workday, a whistle would blow and you'd jump out your window and slide down the tail of a brontosaurus and right into your car like Fred Flintstone.

It'd be considered harmless fun to gather 30 friends, put on horned helmets, and go pillage a nearby town.

Lifeguards could remove citizens from beaches for violating the "public ugliness" ordinance.

Tanks would be far easier to rent.

Garbage would take itself out.

Instead of beer belly, you'd get "beer biceps."

Instead of an expensive engagement ring, you could present your wife-to-be with a giant foam hand that said, "You're #1!"

Valentine's Day would be moved to February 29th so it would only occur in leap years.

On Groundhog Day, if you saw your shadow, you'd get the day off to go drinking. Mother's Day, too. St. Patrick's Day, however, would remain exactly the same. But, it would be celebrated every month.

Cops would be broadcast live, and you could phone in advice to the pursuing cops, or to the crooks.

Two words: Ally McNaked.

Regis and Kathie Lee would be chained to a cement mixer and pushed off the Golden Gate Bridge for the most lucrative pay-per-view event in world history.

The victors in any athletic competition would get to kill and eat the losers.

The only show opposite Monday Night Football would be Monday Night Football From A Different Camera Angle.

It would be perfectly legal to steal a sports car, as long as you returned it the following day with a full tank of gas.

Every man would get four real Get Out of Jail Free cards per year.

When a cop gave you a ticket, every smart-aleck answer you responded with would actually reduce your fine. As in:
Cop: "You know how fast you were going?"
You: "All I know is, I was spilling my beer all over the place."
Cop: "Nice one. That's $10 off."

Faucets would run "Hot," "Cold," and "100 proof."

The Statue of Liberty would get a bright red, 40-foot thong.

People would never talk about how fresh they felt.

Daisy Duke shorts would never again go out of style.

Telephones would automatically cut off after 30 seconds of conversation.

J.D. Heskin

<u>Male Handbook</u>

How many men does it take to open a beer?
None. It should be opened by the time she brings it.

Why is a Laundromat a really bad place to pick up a woman?
Because a woman who can't even afford a washing machine will never be able to support you.

Why do women have smaller feet than men?
So they can stand closer to the kitchen sink.

How do you know when a woman's about to say something smart?
When she starts her sentence with "A man once told me..."

How do you fix a woman's watch?
You don't. There's a clock on the oven!

Why do men pass gas more than women?
Because women won't shut up long enough to build up pressure.

Women are like guns, keep one around long enough and you're gonna want to shoot it.

If your dog is barking at the back door and your wife is yelling at the front door, who do you let in first?
The dog of course...at least he'll shut up after you let him in.

All wives are alike, but they have different faces so you can tell them apart.

What's worse than a Male Chauvinist Pig?
A woman that won't do what she's told.

I married Miss Right. I just didn't know her first name was Always.

I haven't spoken to my wife for 18 months. I don't like to interrupt her.

What do you call a woman who has lost 95% of her intelligence?
Divorced.

Bigamy is having one wife too many. Some say monogamy is the same.

Scientists have discovered a food that diminishes a woman's sex drive by 90%...
Wedding cake.

Marriage is a 3 ring circus: Engagement ring, wedding ring, and suffering.

The last fight was my fault. My wife asked, "What's on the TV?" and I said, "Dust!"

In the beginning, God created earth and rested. Then, God created man and rested. Then, God created woman. Since then, neither God nor man has rested.

My wife and I are inseparable. In fact, last week it took four state troopers and a dog.

Why do men die before their wives?
They want to.

What is the difference between a dog and a fox?
About 5 drinks.

A beggar walked up to a well-dressed woman shopping on Rodeo Drive and said, "I haven't eaten anything in four days." She looked at him and said, "God, I wish I had your willpower."

Do you know the punishment for bigamy?
Two mothers-in-law.

Young Son: Is it true, Dad, I heard that in some parts of Africa a man doesn't know his wife until he marries her?
Dad: That happens in every country, son.

A man put an 'ad' in the classified: "Wife wanted." Next day, he received a hundred letters. They all said the same thing: "You can have mine."

A man meets a genie. The genie tells him he can have whatever he wants, provided that his mother-in-law gets double. The man thinks for a moment and then says, "OK, give me a million dollars and beat me half to death."

The most effective way to remember your wife's birthday is to forget it once.

Women will never be equal to men until they can walk down the street with a bald head and a beer gut, and still think they are beautiful.

Why were shopping carts invented?
To teach women to walk on their hind legs.

How many women does it take to paint a wall?
It depends on how hard you throw them.

What do you call a woman with two brain cells?
Pregnant.

Just Hold Me

Husband and wife are getting all snugly in bed. The passion is heating up. But, then the wife stops and says, "I don't feel like it. I just want you to HOLD me." "Just WHAT!?," stammers the husband. The wife just explains that he is obviously not in tune with her "emotional needs as a WOMAN." The husband realizes that nothing is going to happen tonight and he might as well deal with it. So, the next day, the husband takes her shopping at a big department store. He walks around with her as she tries on three very expensive outfits. She can't decide. He tells his wife to take all three of them, then pick out matching shoes worth $200 each. Finally, they visit the Jewelry Dept where she gets a set of diamond ear rings. The wife is so excited. She goes for the tennis bracelet. The husband says, "You don't even play tennis, but if you like it then let's get it." The wife is so excited she cannot even believe what is going on. She says, "I'm ready to go, let's go to the cash register." The husband says, "Oh no, honey, we're not going to buy all this stuff." The wife's face goes blank. "No honey. I just want you to HOLD this stuff for a while." Her face gets really red and she is about to explode and the Husband says, "You're obviously not in tune with my financial needs as a MAN."

Anything For $100

A man was sitting at a bar enjoying an after-work cocktail when an exceptionally gorgeous and sexy young woman entered. She was so striking that the man could not take his eyes away from her. The young woman noticed his overly-attentive stare and walked directly toward him. Before he could offer his apologies for being so rude, the young woman said to him, "I'll do anything, absolutely anything, that you want me to do, no matter how kinky, for $100 on one condition." Flabbergasted, the man asked what the condition was. The young woman replied, "You have to tell me what you want me to do in just three words." The man considered her proposition for a moment, withdrew his wallet from his pocket and slowly counted out five $20 bills, which he pressed into the young woman's hand. He looked deeply into her eyes and slowly, meaningfully said, "Paint my house."

100 Reasons It's Great To Be A Guy
(According to Women)

1. Phone conversations are over in 30 seconds flat.
2. Movie nudity is virtually always female.
3. You know stuff about tanks.
4. A five-day vacation requires only one suitcase.
5. Monday Night Football.
6. You don't have to monitor your friends sex lives.
7. Your bathroom lines are 80% shorter.
8. You can open all your own jars.
9. Old friends don't give you crap if you've lost or gained weight.
10. Dry cleaners and hair cutters don't rob you blind.

11. When clicking through the channel, you don't have to stall on every shot of someone crying.
12. Your butt is never a factor in a job interview.
13. All your orgasms are real.
14. A beer gut does not make you invisible to the opposite sex.
15. Guys in hockey masks don't attack you.
16. You don't have to lug a bag of useful stuff around everywhere you go.
17. You understand why the movie "Stripes" is funny.
18. You can go to the bathroom without a support group.
19. Your last name stays put.
20. You can leave a hotel bed unmade.
21. When your work is criticized, you don't have to panic that everyone secretly hates you.
22. You can kill your own food.
23. The garage is all yours.
24. You get extra credit for the slightest act of thoughtfulness.
25. You see the humor in Terms of Endearment.
26. Nobody secretly wonders if you swallow.
27. You never have to clean the toilet.
28. You can be showered and ready in 10 minutes.
29. Sex means never worrying about your reputation.
30. Wedding plans take care of themselves.
31. If someone forgets to invite you to something, he or she can still be your friend.
32. Your underwear is $10 for a three pack.
33. The National College Cheerleading Championship
34. None of your co-workers have the power to make you cry.
35. You don't have to shave below your neck.
36. You don't have to curl up next to a hairy butt every night.
37. If you're 34 and single, nobody notices.
38. You can write your name in the snow.
39. You can get into a nontrivial pissing contest.
40. Everything on your face stays its original color.
41. Chocolate is just another snack.
42. You can be president.
43. You can quietly enjoy a car ride from the passenger seat.
44. Flowers fix everything.
45. You never have to worry about other people's feelings.
46. You get to think about sex 90% of your waking hours.
47. You can wear a white shirt to a water park.
48. Three pair of shoes are more than enough.
49. You can eat a banana in a hardware store.
50. You can say anything and not worry about what people think.
51. Foreplay is optional.
52. Michael Bolton doesn't live in your universe.
53. Nobody stops telling a good dirty joke when you walk into the room.
54. You can whip your shirt off on a hot day.
55. You don't have to clean your apartment if the meter reader is coming by.

56. You never feel compelled to stop a pal from getting laid.
57. Car mechanics tell you the truth.
58. You don't give a rat's ass if someone notices your new haircut.
59. You can watch a game in silence with your buddy for hours without even thinking "He must be mad at me."
60. The world is your urinal.
61. You never drop innocuous statements to mean your lover is about to leave you.
62. You get to jump up and slap stuff.
63. Hot wax never comes near your pubic area.
64. One mood, all the time.
65. You can admire Clint Eastwood without starving yourself to look like him.
66. You never have to drive to another gas station because this one's just to skeevy.
67. You know at least 20 ways to open a beer bottle.
68. You can sit with your knees apart no matter what you are wearing.
69. Same work....more pay.
70. Gray hair and wrinkles add character.
71. You don't have to leave the room to make an emergency crotch adjustment.
72. Wedding Dress $2000; Tux rental $100.
73. You don't care if someone is talking about you behind your back.
74. With 400 million sperm per shot, you could double the earth's population in 15 tries, at least in theory.
75. You don't mooch off others' desserts.
76. If you retain water, it's in a canteen.
77. The remote is yours and yours alone.
78. People never glance at your chest when your talking to them.
79. ESPN's sports center.
80. You can drop by to see a friend without bringing a little gift.
81. Bachelor parties kick butt over bridal showers.
82. You have a normal and healthy relationship with your mother.
83. You can buy condoms without the shopkeeper imagining you naked.
84. You needn't pretend you're "freshening up" to go to the bathroom.
85. If you don't call your buddy when you say you will, he won't tell your friends you've changed.
86. Someday you'll be a dirty old man.
87. You can rationalize any behavior with the handy phrase, "Screw it!"
88. If another guy shows up at the party in the same outfit, you might become lifelong buddies.
89. Princess Di's death was almost just another obituary.
90. The occasional well-rendered belch is practically expected.
91. You never have to miss a sexual opportunity because you're not in the mood.
92. You think the idea of punting a small dog is funny.
93. If something mechanical didn't work, you can bash it with a hammer and throw it across the room.
94. New shoes don't cut, blister, or mangle your feet.
95. Porn movies are designed with your mind in mind.
96. You don't have to remember everyone's birthdays and anniversaries.
97. Not liking a person does not preclude having great sex with them.

98. Your pals can be trusted never to trap you with, "So... notice anything different?"
99. Baywatch
100. There is always a game on somewhere.

The Beer Prayer

Our lager,
Which art in barrels,
Hallowed be thy drink.
Thy will be drunk. I will be drunk,
At home as it is in the pub.
Give us this day our foamy head,
And forgive us our spillage,
As we forgive those who spill against us.
And lead us not into incarceration,
But deliver us from hangovers,
For thine is the beer, the bitter, and the lager.
Forever and ever.
BARMEN.

3 Girlfriends And $5000

There is a man who has three girlfriends, but he does not know which one to marry. So, he decides to give each one $5000 and see how each of them spends it. The first one goes out and gets a total makeover with the money. She gets new clothes, a new hairdo, manicure, pedicure, the works, and tells the man, "I spent the money so I could look pretty for you because I love you so much." The second one went out and bought new golf clubs, a CD player, a television, and a stereo and gives them to the man. She says, "I bought these gifts for you with the money because I love you so much." The third one takes the $5000 and invests it in the stock market, doubles her investment, returns the $5000 to the man and reinvests the rest. She says, "I am investing the rest of the money for our future because I love you so much." The man thought long and hard about how each of the women spent the money, and decided to marry the one with the biggest breasts.

Ticket To Pittsburg

A group of young businessmen were chatting at the bar, and decides to share his recent embarrassment with the others. He tells them that he was booking a plane ticket to Pittsburgh, but he was so preoccupied with the beautiful breasts of the girl to the counter, that instead of saying "I'd like a ticket to Pittsburgh," he said, "I'd like a picket to Titsburg!" An older guy nearby hears the story and says, "You know, I had a similar experience with my wife this morning. We were sitting at the breakfast table and I meant to say, "Darling, could you please pass the butter" ... but what came out was, "You bitch, you're ruining my frickin' life!"

What Men Really Mean

"I'm going fishing."
Really means..."I'm going to drink myself dangerously stupid, and stand by a stream
           with a stick in my hand, while the fish swim by in complete safety."

"It's a guy thing."
Really means..."There is no rational thought pattern connected with it, and you have
           no chance at all of making it logical."

"Can I help with dinner?"
Really means..."Why isn't it already on the table?"

"Uh huh," "Sure, honey," or "Yes, dear."
Really means...Absolutely nothing. It's a conditioned response.

"It would take too long to explain."
Really means..."I have no idea how it works."

"We're going to be late."
Really means..."Now I have a legitimate excuse to drive like a maniac."

"I was listening to you. It's just that I have things on my mind."
Really means..."I was wondering if that red-head over there is wearing a bra."

"Take a break, honey, you're working too hard."
Really means..."I can't hear the game over the vacuum cleaner."

"That's interesting, dear."
Really means..."Are you still talking?"

It's a really good movie."
Really means..."It's got guns, knives, fast cars, and beautiful women."

"That's women's work."
Really means..."It's difficult, dirty, and thankless."

"You know how bad my memory is."
Really means..."I remember the theme song to 'F Troop,' the address of the first girl
           I ever kissed and the VIN of every car I've ever owned, but I
           forgot your birthday."

"I was just thinking about you, and got you these roses."
Really means..."The girl selling them on the corner was a real babe."

What Men Really Mean, Part II

"Oh, don't fuss. I just cut myself, it's no big deal."
Really means…"I have actually severed a limb, but will bleed to death before I admit I'm hurt."

"Hey, I've got my reasons for what I'm doing."
Really means…"And, I sure hope I think of some pretty soon."

"I can't find it."
Really means…"It didn't fall into my outstretched hands, so I'm completely clueless."

"What did I do this time?"
Really means…"What did you catch me at?"

"I heard you."
Really means…"I haven't the foggiest clue what you just said, and am hoping desperately that I can fake it well enough so that you don't spend the next 3 days yelling at me."

"You know I could never love anyone else."
Really means…"I am used to the way you yell at me, and realize it could be worse."

"You look terrific."
Really means…"Oh, God, please don't try on one more outfit. I'm starving."

"I'm not lost. I know exactly where we are."
Really means…"No one will ever see us alive again."

"We share the housework."
Really means…"I make the messes, she cleans them up."

Cowboy Logic

Don't squat with your spurs on.

Good judgment comes from experience, and a lot of that comes from bad judgment.

Lettin' the cat outta the bag is a whole lot easier 'n puttin' it back in.

If you're ridin' ahead of the herd, take a look back every now and then to make sure it's still there.

If you get to thinkin' you're a person of some influence, try orderin' somebody else's dog around.

After eating an entire bull, a mountain lion felt so good, he started roaring. He kept it up until a hunter came along and shot him...The moral: When you're full of bull, keep your mouth shut.

Never kick a cow chip on a hot day.

There's two theories to arguin' with a woman. Neither one works.

If you find yourself in a hole, the first thing to do is stop diggin'.

Never slap a man who's chewin' tobacco.

It don't take a genius to spot a goat in a flock of sheep.

Always drink upstream from the herd.

When you give a lesson in meanness to a critter or a person, don't be surprised if they learn their lesson.

When you're throwin' your weight around, be ready to have it thrown around by somebody else.

The quickest way to double yer money is to fold it over and put it back in yer pocket.

Never miss a good chance to shut up.

There are three kinds of men. The one that learns by reading. The few who learn by observation. The rest of them have to pee on the electric fence for themselves.

4 Guys Telling Stories

Four guys are telling stories in a bar. One guy leaves for a bathroom break. Three guys are left..... First guy says, "I was worried that my son was gonna be a loser because he started out washing cars for a local dealership. Turns out that he got a break, they made him a salesman, and he sold so many cars that he bought the dealership. In fact, he's so successful that he just gave his best friend a new Mercedes for his birthday." Second guy says, "I was worried about my son too because he started out raking leaves for a Realtor. Turns out, HE got a break, they made him a commissioned salesman, and he eventually bought the real estate firm. In fact, HE's so successful that he just gave his best friend a new house for his birthday." Third guy says, "Yeah, I hear you. MY son started out sweeping floors in a brokerage firm. Well, HE got a break, they made HIM a broker, and now he owns the brokerage firm. In fact, he's so rich that he just gave HIS best friend $1million in stock for his birthday." Fourth guy comes back from the can. The first 3 explain that they are telling stories about their kids so he says, "Well, I'm embarrassed to admit that my son is a MAJOR disappointment. He started out as a hairdresser and is STILL a hairdresser after 15 years. In fact I just found out that he's gay and has SEVERAL boyfriends. But, I try to look at the bright side; his boyfriends just bought him a new Mercedes, a new house and $1 million in stock for his birthday."

If Men Were To Rewrite The Rules

Rule #1: Anything we said six or eight months ago is inadmissible in an argument. All comments become null and void after seven days.

Rule #2: If you don't want to dress like Victoria's Secret girls, don't expect us to act like soap opera guys.

Rule #3: If we say something that can be interpreted in two ways, and one of the ways makes you sad or angry, we meant the other way.

Rule #4: It is in neither your best interest or ours to make us take those stupid Cosmo quizzes together.

Rule #5: Let us ogle. If we don't look at other women how can we know how pretty you are?

Rule #6: Don't rub the lamp if you don't want the genie to come out.

Rule #7: You can either ask us to do something OR tell us how you want it done - not both.

Rule #8: Whenever possible, please say whatever you have to say during commercials.

Rule #9: Christopher Columbus didn't need directions and neither do we.

Rule #10: Women who wear Wonder bras and low-cut blouses lose their right to complain about having their boobs stared at.

Rule #11: When we're turning the wheel and the car is nosing onto the off ramp, you saying, "This is our exit" is not necessary.

Rule #12: Don't fake it. We'd rather be ineffective than deceived.

Email This!

<u>Kids</u>

A Young Brave

A young brave was being inducted through his manhood ceremony to join the warriors of the tribe. He was faced with 3 tents. In the first one was a gallon of plum wine, which he had to drink in one go. In the second was a mountain lion with toothache, from which he had to remove the painful tooth. In the third was a woman who had never had an orgasm, etc., etc. He entered the first tent, and after a while staggered out, very drunk, holding the empty wine skin. The warriors all applauded. He staggered into the second tent with the tribe all holding their breath. There were terrible screams and growls, which got worse and worse as time went on, culminating in such a loud shriek that the tribesmen were all convinced he must be dead. But, finally he staggered out, bruised and bleeding, and said, "Now take me to the woman with a toothache."

What Is Politics?

A little boy goes to his dad and asks, "What is politics?" Dad says, "Well son, it is confusing, but let me try to explain it this way: I'm the bread winner of the family, so let's call me Capitalism. Your Mom, she's the administrator of the money, so we'll call her the Government. We're here to take care of your needs, so we'll call you the People. The nanny, we'll consider her the Working Class. Your baby brother, we'll call him the Future. Now, think about that and see if that makes sense. So, the little boy goes off to bed thinking about what Dad has said. Later that night, he hears his baby brother crying, he gets up to check on him. He finds that the baby has severely soiled his diaper. The little boy goes to his parents' room and finds his mother sound asleep. Not wanting to wake her, he goes to the nanny's room. Finding the door locked, he peeks in the keyhole and sees his father in bed with the nanny. He gives up and goes back to bed. The next morning, the little boy says to his father, "Dad, I think I understand the concept of politics now." The father says, "Good, son tell me in your own words what you think politics is all about." The little boy replies, "Well, while Capitalism is screwing the Working Class, the Government is sound asleep, the People are being ignored and the Future is in deep crap."

Definitely

A nursery school teacher says to her class, "Who can use the word 'definitely' in a sentence?" First little girl says, "The sky is definitely blue." The teacher says, "Sorry Amy, but the sky can be gray, or orange depending on the weather." Second, a little boy says, "Trees are definitely green." "Sorry, but in the autumn many trees are brown or gold," said the teacher. Little Johnny, from the back of the class, stands up and asks, "Does a fart have lumps?" The teacher looks horrified and says, "Johnny! That's disgusting. Of course not!!!" "OK... then I have DEFINITELY crapped my pants," said Johnny.

Wee Ones

In the back woods of Arkansas, Mr. Stewart's wife went into labor in the middle of the night, and the doctor was called out to assist in the delivery. To keep the nervous father-to-be busy, the doctor handed him a lantern and said, "Here, you hold this high so I can see what I'm doing." Soon, a wee baby boy was brought into the world. "Whoa there Scotty!" said the doctor. "Don't be in a rush to put the lantern down...I think there's yet another wee one to come." Sure enough, within minutes he had delivered a wee bonnie lass. "No, no, don't be in a great hurry to be putting down that lantern, lad...It seems there's yet another one besides!" cried the doctor. The Scot scratched his head in bewilderment, and asked the doctor, "Do ye think it's the light that's attractin' them?"

The Train

A mother was working in the kitchen listening to her son playing with his new electric train in the living room. She heard the train stop, and her son said, "All of you sons of bitches who want to get off, get the hell off now, cause this is the last stop! And, all you sons of bitches who are returning and want to get on, get your asses on the train now, cause we're going down the tracks!" The mother went into the living room and told her son, "We don't use that kind of language in this house. Now go to your room and stay there for TWO HOURS. When you come out, you may go back and play with your train, but only if you use nice language." Two hours later, the boy came out of the bedroom and resumed playing with his train. Soon, the train stopped and the mother heard her son say "All passengers who are disembarking the train, please remember to take all of your belongings with you. We thank you for riding with us today and hope your trip was a pleasant one. We hope you will ride with us again soon." She hears the little boy continue, "For those of you just boarding, we ask you to stow all of your hand luggage under your seat. Remember, there is no smoking on the train. We hope you will have a pleasant and relaxing journey with us today." Then, the child added, "And, for those of you who are pissed off about the TWO HOUR delay, see the bitch in the kitchen."

A Horseback Christmas

On Christmas morning, a cop on horseback is sitting at a traffic light, and next to him is a kid on his shiny new bike. The cop says to the kid, "Nice bike you got there. Did Santa bring that to you?" The kid says, "Yeah." The cop says, "Well, next year tell Santa to put a tail-light on that bike." The cop then proceeds to issue the kid a $20.00 bicycle safety violation ticket. The kid takes the ticket and before he rides off says, "By the way, that's a nice horse you got there. Did Santa bring that to you?" Humoring the kid, the cop says, "Yeah, he sure did." The kid says, "Well, next year tell Santa to put the dick underneath the horse instead of on top."

Cheerios

A 7 year old boy and his 4 year old brother were upstairs in their bedroom. The 7 year old was explaining that it was high time that the two of them begin swearing. When his little brother responded enthusiastically, the 7 year old hatched the plan, "When we go downstairs for breakfast this morning, I'll say 'Hell' and you say 'fat ass.' The 4 year old happily agreed. As the two boys were seating themselves at the breakfast table, their mother walked in and asked her older son what he would like to eat for breakfast. The 7 year old replied, "Ah hell, Mom, I'll just have some Cheerios." "WHACK!" The surprised mother reacted quickly. The boy ran upstairs, bawling and rubbing his behind. With a sterner voice, the mother then turned to the younger son, "And, what would YOU like for breakfast?" "I don't know," the 4 year old blubbered, "but you can bet your fat ass it's not gonna be Cheerios."

The Key Is Effective Communications

According to a radio report, a middle school in Oregon was faced with a unique problem. A number of girls were beginning to use lipstick and would put it on in the bathroom. That was fine, but after they put on their lipstick they would press their lips to the mirrors leaving dozens of little lip prints. Finally, the principal decided that something had to be done. She called all the girls to the bathroom and met them there with the custodian. She explained that all these lip prints were causing a major problem for the custodian who had to clean the mirrors every day. To demonstrate how difficult it was to clean the mirrors, she asked the custodian to clean one of the mirrors. He proceeded to take out a long-handled brush, dip it into the nearest toilet and scrub the mirror. Since then, there have been no lip prints on the mirror.

A Boy From Minnesota

There once was a boy who worked in the produce section of the market. One day, a man came in and asked to buy half a head of lettuce. The boy told him that they only sold whole heads of lettuce, but the man replied that he did not need a whole head, only a half head. The boy said he would ask his manager about the matter. The boy walked into the back room and said, "There is some idiot out there who wants to buy only a half a head of lettuce." As he was finishing saying this he turned around to find the man standing behind him, so he added, "And, this gentleman wants to buy the other half." The manager okayed the deal and the man went on his way. Later, the manager said to the boy, "You almost got yourself in a lot of trouble earlier, but I must say I was impressed with the way you got yourself out of it. You think on your feet, and we like that here in Mt View. Where are you from, son?" The boy replied, "Minnesota, sir." "Oh really? Why did you leave Minnesota?" asked the manager. The boy replied, "Minnesotans are just a bunch of whores and hockey players." The manager was shocked and replied, "My wife is from Minnesota!" The boy answered, "Really? What team did she play for?"

Kids On Proverbs

A first grade teacher collected old, well known proverbs. She gave each kid in her class the first half of a proverb and had them come up with the rest.

As You Shall Make Your Bed So Shall You..... Mess It Up.

Better Be Safe Than......................... Punch A 5th Grader.

A Miss Is As Good As A...................... Mr.

Strike While The............................ Bug Is Close.

It's Always Darkest Before.................. Daylight Savings Time.

Never Under Estimate The Power Of........... Termites.

You Can't Teach An Old Dog New.............. Math.

If You Lie Down With The Dogs, You'll....... Stink In The Morning.

An Idle Mind Is............................. The Best Way To Relax.

Where There's Smoke, There's................ Pollution.

A Penny Saved Is............................ Not Much.

Two's Company, Three's...................... The Musketeers.

Don't Put Off Until Tomorrow What........... You Put On To Go To Bed.

Laugh And The Whole World Laughs With You, Cry And.........You Have To Blow Your Nose.

None Are So Blind As........................ Helen Keller.

Children Should Be Seen And Not............. Spanked Or Grounded.

If At First You Don't Succeed............... Get New Batteries.

When The Blind Leadeth The Blind............ Get Out Of The Way.

Don't Bite The Hand That.................... Looks Dirty.

You Can Lead A Horse To Water But........... How?

Kids On Love And Wisdom

Questions concerning love and wisdom were posed to a group of children ages 5 to 10. Their responses were amazingly astute and very enlightening, thus proving that all we need to know, we probably learned in kindergarten.

WHAT IS THE PROPER AGE TO GET MARRIED?
"Eighty-four. Because at that age, you don't have to work anymore, and you can spend all your time loving each other in your bedroom." (Judy, 8)

"Once I'm done with kindergarten, I'm going to find me a wife." (Tommy, 5)

WHAT DO MOST PEOPLE DO ON A DATE?
"On the first date, they just tell each other lies, and that usually gets them interested enough to go for a second date." (Mike, 10)

WHEN IS IT OKAY TO KISS SOMEONE?
"You should never kiss a girl unless you have enough bucks to buy her a big ring and her own VCR, 'cause she'll want to have videos of the wedding." (Jim, 10)

"Never kiss in front of other people. It's a big embarrassing thing if anybody sees you. But, if nobody sees you, I might be willing to try it with a handsome boy, but just for a few hours." (Kally, 9)

IS IT BETTER TO BE SINGLE OR MARRIED?
"It's better for girls to be single, but not for boys. Boys need somebody to clean up after them." (Lynette, 9)

"It gives me a headache to think about that stuff. I'm just a kid. I don't need that kind of trouble." (Kenny, 7)

CONCERNING WHY LOVE HAPPENS BETWEEN TWO PEOPLE:
"No one is sure why it happens, but I heard it has something to do with how you smell. That's why perfume and deodorant are so popular." (Jan, 9)

"I think you're supposed to get shot with an arrow or something, but the rest of it isn't supposed to be so painful." (Harlen, 8)

ON WHAT FALLING IN LOVE IS LIKE:
"Like an avalanche where you have to run for your life." (Roger, 9)

"If falling in love is anything like learning to spell, I don't want to do it. It takes to long to learn." (Leo, 7)

ON THE ROLE OF GOOD LOOKS IN LOVE AND ROMANCE:
"If you want to be loved by somebody who isn't already in your family, it doesn't hurt to be beautiful." (Jeanne, 8)

"It isn't always just how you look. Look at me. I'm handsome like anything and I haven't got anybody to marry me yet." (Gary, 7)

"Beauty is skin deep. But, how rich you are can last a longtime." (Christine, 9)

CONCERNING WHY LOVERS OFTEN HOLD HANDS:
"They want to make sure their rings don't fall off, because they paid good money for them." (David, 8)

CONFIDENTIAL OPINIONS ABOUT LOVE:
"I'm in favor of love as long as it doesn't happen when 'The Simpsons' are on TV." (Anita, 6)

"Love will find you, even if you are trying to hide from it. I've been trying to hide from it since I was five, but the girls keep finding me." (Bobby, 8)

"I'm not rushing into being in love. I'm finding fourth grade hard enough." (Regina, 10)

PERSONAL QUALITIES NECESSARY TO BE A GOOD LOVER:
"One of you should know how to write a check. Because, even if you have tons of love, there is still going to be a lot of bills." (Ava, 8)

SOME SUREFIRE WAYS TO MAKE A PERSON FALL IN LOVE WITH YOU:
"Tell them that you own a whole bunch of candy stores." (Del, 6)

"Don't do things like have smelly, green sneakers. You might get attention, but attention ain't the same thing as love." (Alonzo, 9)

"One way is to take the girl out to eat. Make sure it's something she likes to eat. French fries usually works for me." (Bart, 9)

HOW CAN YOU TELL IF TWO ADULTS EATING DINNER AT A RESTAURANT ARE IN LOVE?
"Just see if the man picks up the check. That's how you can tell if he's in love." (John, 9)

"Lovers will just be staring at each other and their food will get cold. Other people care more about the food," (Brad, 8)

"It's love if they order one of those desserts that are on fire. They like to order those because it's just like their hearts are on fire." (Christine, 9)

WHAT MOST PEOPLE ARE THINKING WHEN THEY SAY "I LOVE YOU":
"The person is thinking: Yeah, I really do love him, but I hope he showers at least once a day." (Michelle, 9)

HOW A PERSON LEARNS TO KISS:
"You learn it right on the spot, when the gooshy feelings get the best of you." (Doug, 7)

"It might help if you watched soap operas all day." (Carin, 9)

WHEN IS IT OKAY TO KISS SOMEONE?
"It's never okay to kiss a boy. They always slobber all over you...that's why I stopped doing it." (Jean, 10)

HOW TO MAKE LOVE ENDURE:
"Spend most of your time loving instead of going to work." (Tom, 7)

"Don't forget your wife's name...that will mess up the love." (Roger, 8)

"Be a good kisser. It might make your wife forget that you never take the trash out." (Randy, 8)

Dear Dad

Dear Dad,

$chool i$ really great. I am making lot$ of friend$ and $tudying very hard. With all my $tuff, I $imply can't think of anything I need., $o, if you would like, you can ju$t $end me a card, a$ I would love to hear from you.

Love,
Your $on.

Dear Son,

I kNOw that astroNOmy, ecoNOmics, and oceaNOgraphy are eNOugh to keep even an hoNOr student busy. Do NOt forget that the pursuit of kNOwledge is a NOble task, and you can never study eNOugh.

Love,
Dad

Next Time Go With A Flower Girl...

A little boy was in a relative's wedding. As he was coming down the aisle he would take two steps, stop, and turn to the crowd (alternating between bride's side and groom's side). While facing the crowd, he would put his hands up like claws and roar. So it went, step, step, ROAR, step, step, ROAR all the way down the aisle. As you can imagine, the crowd was near tears from laughing so hard by the time he reached the pulpit. The little boy, however, was getting more and more distressed from all the laughing, and was also near tears by the time he reached the pulpit. When asked what he was doing, the child sniffed and said, "I was being the Ring Bear!"

Miraculous Conception

A woman takes her 16-year-old daughter to the doctor. The doctor says, "Okay, Mrs. Jones, what's the problem?" The mother says, "It's my daughter, Debbie. She keeps getting these cravings, she's putting on weight, and is sick most mornings." The doctor gives Debbie a good examination, then turns to the mother and says, "Well, I don't know how to tell you this, but your Debbie is pregnant...about 4 months, would be my guess." The mother says, "Pregnant?! She can't be, she has never ever been left alone with a man! Have you, Debbie?" Debbie says, "No mother! I've never even kissed a man!" The doctor walked over to the window and just stares out it. About five minutes pass and finally the mother says, "Is there something wrong out there doctor?" The doctor replies, "No, not really, it's just that the last time anything like this happened, a star appeared in the east and three wise men came over the hill. I'll be damned if I'm going to miss it this time!"

Wild Temper Tantrum

As the crowded airliner is about to take off, the peace is shattered by a five-year-old boy who picks that moment to throw a wild temper tantrum. No matter what his frustrated, embarrassed mother does to try to calm him down, the boy continues to scream furiously and kick the seats around him. Suddenly, from the rear of the plane, an elderly man in the uniform of an Air Force General is seen slowly walking forward up the aisle. Stopping the flustered mother with an upraised hand, the white-haired, courtly, soft-spoken General leans down and, motioning toward his chest, whispers something into the boy's ear. Instantly, the boy calms down, gently takes his mother's hand, and quietly fastens his seat belt. All the other passengers burst into spontaneous applause. As the General slowly makes his way back to his seat, one of the cabin attendants touches his sleeve. "Excuse me, General," she asks quietly, "but could I ask you what magic words you used on that little boy?" The old man smiles serenely and gently confides, "I showed him my pilot's wings, service stars, and battle ribbons, and explained that they entitle me to throw one passenger out the plane door, on any flight I choose."

J.D. Heskin

Letter From Camp

Dear Mom,

Our scout master told us all write to our parents in case you saw the flood on TV and worried. We are OK. Only 1 of our tents and 2 sleeping bags got washed away. Luckily, none of us got drowned because we were all up on the mountain looking for Chad when it happened. Oh yes, please call Chad's mother and tell her he is OK. He can't write because of the cast. I got to ride in one of the search and rescue jeeps. It was neat. We never would have found him in the dark if it hadn't been for the lightning. Scoutmaster Webb got mad at Chad for going on a hike alone without telling anyone. Chad said he did tell him, but it was during the fire so he probably didn't hear him. Did you know that if you put gas on a fire, the gas can will blow up? The wet wood still didn't burn, but one of our tents did. Also, some of our clothes. John is going to look weird until his hair grows back.

We will be home on Saturday if Scoutmaster Webb gets the car fixed. It wasn't his fault about the wreck. The brakes worked OK when we left. Scoutmaster Webb said that a car that old you have to expect something to break down; that's probably why he can't get insurance on it. We think it's a neat car. He doesn't care if we get it dirty, and if it's hot, sometimes he lets us ride on the tailgate. It gets pretty hot with 10 people in a car. He let us take turns riding in the trailer until the highway patrolman stopped and talked to us. Scoutmaster Webb is a neat guy. Don't worry, he is a good driver. In fact, he is teaching Terry how to drive. But, he only lets him drive on the mountain roads where there isn't any traffic. All we ever see up there are logging trucks. This morning all of the guys were diving off the rocks and swimming out in the lake. Scoutmaster Webb wouldn't let me because I can't swim and Chad was afraid he would sink because of his cast, so he let us take the canoe across the lake. It was great. You can still see some of the trees under the water from the flood.

Scoutmaster Webb isn't crabby like some scoutmasters. He didn't even get mad about the life jackets. He has to spend a lot of time working on the car so we are trying not to cause him any trouble. Guess what? We have all passed our first aid merit badges. When Dave dove in the lake and cut his arm, we got to see how a tourniquet works. Also, Wade and I threw up. Scoutmaster Webb said it probably was just food poisoning from the leftover chicken. He said they got sick that way with the food they ate in prison. I'm so glad he got out and became our scoutmaster. He said he sure figured out how to get things done better while he was doing his time. I have to go now. We are going into town to mail our letters and buy bullets. Don't worry about anything. We are fine.

Love,
Travis :)

Pregnant Woman In Coma

A single, pregnant woman gets in a car accident and falls into deep coma. Asleep for nearly 6 months, she wakes up, realizes that she is no longer pregnant and frantically asks the doctor about her baby. The doctor replies, "Ma'am you had twins! A boy and a girl. Your brother from Wisconsin came in and named them." The woman thinks to herself, "No, not my brother... he's an idiot!" She asks the doctor, "Well, what's the girl's name?" "Denise," replies the Doctor. "Wow, that's not a bad name, I like it! What's the boy's name?" she asks. To which, the Doctor replies, "Denephew."

Why Parents Get Gray

The boss of a big company needed to call one of his employees about an urgent problem with one of the main computers. He dialed the employee's phone number and was greeted with a child's whispered, "Hello?" Feeling put out at the inconvenience of having to talk to a youngster the boss asked, "Is your Daddy home?" "Yes," whispered the small voice. "May I talk with him?" the man asked. To the surprise of the boss, the small voice whispered, "No." Wanting to talk with an adult, the boss asked, "Is your Mommy there?" Again the small voice whispered, "no." Knowing that it was not likely that a young child would be left home alone, the boss decided he would just leave a message with the person watching over the child. "Is there any one there the boss asked the child. "Yes" whispered the child, "A policeman." Wondering what a cop would be doing at his employee's home, the boss asked, "May I speak with the policeman?" "No, he's busy," whispered the child. "Busy doing what?" asked the boss. "Talking to Daddy and Mommy and the Fireman," came the whispered answer. Growing concerned and even worried as he heard what sounded like a helicopter through the ear piece on the phone the boss asked, "What is that noise?" "A hello-copper," answered the whispering voice. "What is going on there?" asked the boss, now alarmed. In an awed whispering voice the child answered, "The search team just landed the hello-copper." Alarmed, concerned and more than just a little frustrated the boss asked, "Why are they there?" Still whispering, the young voice replied along with a muffled giggle, "They're looking for me."

Medicine

Zachary Disease

A woman was very despondent over not having met a guy in quite some time. She was becoming agitated and worried that she might never find a mate. In hopes of finding a solution to her problem, she decided that it was time to see a doctor. Looking through the phone book, she came upon a Chinese doctor, a sex therapist, named Dr. Chang. When the woman arrived, she told the doctor her symptoms, and he said, "Take off aw you crothes and you crawl real fass away from me across the froor." She crawled to the other side of the room and Dr. Chang said, "Now, you craw real fass back to me," and she did. Dr. Chang shook his head and said, "You haf real bad case of Zachary Disease....worse case I ever see! That why you haf sex probrem." The woman was completely confused and asked the doctor exactly what Zachary Disease was. He replied, "Zachary Disease: that when you face rook ZACHARY rike you ass!"

Fred's Castration

Fred goes to a doctor and says, "Doc, I want to be castrated." The doctor says, "Look, I don't know what kind of cult you're into or what your motives are, but I'm not going to do that sort of operation." Fred replies, "Doc, I just want to be castrated and I'm a little embarrassed about talking about it, but I have $5,000 cash right here. Will you do it?" The doctor says, "Well, okay, I guess I could make this one exception. I don't understand it, but all right." He puts Fred to sleep, does the operation and is waiting at the bedside when Fred wakes up. "Well, Doc, how'd it go?" Fred asks. "It went fine, just fine. It's really not too difficult of an operation. As a matter of fact, $5,000 is a lot to pay for such a simple task and I felt a little guilty about taking that much. So, while I was operating, I also noticed that you had never been circumcised, so I went ahead and did that, too. I think, it's really better for a man to be circumcised, and I hope you don't mind my..." "Circumcised!" yells Fred. "That's the word!"

The Brain Transplant

The patient's family gathered to hear what the specialists had to say. "Things don't look good." The only chance is a brain transplant. This is an experimental procedure. It might work, but the bad news is that brains are very expensive, and you will have to pay the costs yourselves." "Well, how much does a brain cost?" asked the relatives. "For a male brain, $500,000. For a female brain, $200,000." Some of the younger male relatives tried to look shocked, but all the men nodded because they thought they understood. A few actually smirked. But, the patient's daughter was unsatisfied and asked, "Why the difference in price between male brains and female brains?" "A standard pricing practice," said the head of the team. "Women's brains have to be marked down because they have actually been used."

A Pharmacist

A girl asks her boyfriend to come over Friday night and have dinner with her parents. Since this is such a big event, the girl announces her boyfriend that after dinner, she would like to go out and have sex for the first time. Well, the boy is ecstatic, but he has never had sex before, so he takes a trip to the pharmacist to get some condoms. The pharmacist helps the boy for about an hour. He tells the boy everything there is to know about condoms and sex. At the register, the pharmacist asks the boy how many condoms he'd like to buy, a 3-pack, 10 pack, or family pack. The boy insists on the family pack because he thinks he will be rather busy, it being his first time and all. That night, the boy shows up at the girls parents house and meets his girlfriend at the door. "Oh, I'm so excited for you to meet my parents. Come on in!" The boy goes inside and is taken to the dinner table where the girls parents are seated. The boy quickly offers to say grace and bows his head. A minute passes, and the boy is still in deep prayer with his head down. Ten minutes pass, and still no movement from the boy. Finally, after 20 minutes with his head down, the girlfriend finally leans over and whispers to the boyfriend, "I had no idea you were this religious." The boy turns and whispers back, "I had no idea your father was a pharmacist."

The Witch Doctor

A man had been troubled by his inability to achieve an erection. After visiting numerous doctors without help, he decided to consult a witch doctor. The witch doctor threw some herbs in the fire, shook his rattle and danced wildly. When he was through he said, "I have placed a powerful spell on you, but it will only work once a year. When you are ready just say...1, 2, 3 and you will get the largest erection that you have ever had. After your wife has been satisfied she simply has to say...1, 2, 3, 4 and it will be gone for one year." Later that night as the man lay in bed he said to his wife, "Watch this! 1, 2, 3." He sprang to life larger and stiffer then ever before. His wife was amazed, smiled, and said, "That's great! But, what did you say 1, 2, 3 for?"

Dr. Howard

Howard had felt guilty all day long. No matter how much he tried to forget about it, he couldn't. The guilt and sense of betrayal were overwhelming. But, every once in a while he'd hear that soothing voice trying to reassure him, "Howard, don't worry about it. You aren't the first doctor to sleep with one of his patients and you won't be the last." But, invariably the other voice would bring him back to reality, "But Howard, you're a veterinarian."

Viagra Spin-Offs

With Viagra such a hit, Pfizer is bringing forth a whole line of drugs oriented towards improving the performance of men in today's society...

DIRECTRA: A dose of this drug given to men before leaving on car trips caused 72 percent of them to stop and ask directions when they got lost, compared to a control group of 0.2 percent.

PROJECTRA: Men given this experimental new drug were far more likely to actually finish a household repair project before starting a new one.

CHILDAGRA: Men taking this drug reported a sudden, overwhelming urge to perform more child-care tasks, especially, cleaning up spills and "little accidents."

COMPLIMENTRA: In clinical trials, 82 percent of middle-aged men administered this drug noticed that their wives had a new hairstyle. Currently being tested to see if its effects extend to noticing new clothing.

BUYAGRA: Married and otherwise attached men reported a sudden urge to buy their sweeties expensive jewelry and gifts after talking this drug for only two days. Still to be seen, whether the drug can be continued for a period longer than your favorites store's return limit.

NEGA-VIAGRA: Has the exact opposite effect of Viagra. Currently undergoing clinical trials on sitting U.S. presidents.

NAGA-SPORTAGRA: This drug had the strange effect of making men want to turn off televised sports and actually converse with other family members.

FLATULAGRA: This complex drug converts men's noxious intestinal gases back into food solids. Special bonus: Dosage can be doubled for long car rides.

FLYAGRA: This drug has been showing great promise in treating men with O.F.D. (Open Fly Disorder). Especially useful for men on Viagra.

PRYAGRA: About to fail its clinical trial, this drug gave men in the test group an irresistible urge to dig into the personal affairs of other people.
Note: Apparent over-dose turned three test subjects into "special prosecutors."

LIAGRA: This drug causes men to be less than truthful when being asked about their sexual affairs. Will be available in Regular, Grand Jury and Presidential Strength versions.

How To Keep A Healthy Level Of Sanity While Driving Other People Insane

1. Page yourself over the intercom. (Don't disguise your voice!)

2. Find out where your boss shops and buy exactly the same outfits. Always wear them one day after your boss does. (This is especially effective if your boss is the opposite gender.)

3. Send e-mail to the rest of the company to tell them what you're doing. For example: 'If anyone needs me, I'll be in the bathroom.'

4. While sitting at your desk, soak your fingers in Palmolive.

5. Put mosquito netting around your cubicle.

6. Insist that your e-mail address be zena-goddess-of-FIRE@companyname.com

7. Every time someone asks you to do something, ask if they want fries with that.

8. Suggest that the Coke machine be filled with beer.

9. Encourage your colleagues to join you in a little synchronized chair dancing.

10. Put your garbage can on your desk and label it "IN."

11. Develop an unnatural fear of staplers.

12. Put decaf in the coffeemaker for 3 weeks. Once everyone has gotten over their caffeine addictions, switch to espresso.

13. In the memo field of all your checks, write "for sexual favors."

14. When driving colleagues around, insist on keeping your car's windshield wipers running during all weather conditions to keep them tuned up.

15. Reply to everything someone says with, "That's what you think."

16. Practice making fax and modem noises.

17. Finish all your sentences with "in accordance with the prophecy."

18. Adjust the tint on your monitor so that the brightness level lights the entire working area. Insist to others that you like it that way.

19. As often as possible, skip rather than walk.

20. Ask people what sex they are.

21. While making presentations, occasionally bob your head like a parakeet.

22. At lunch time, sit in your parked car and point a hair dryer at passing cars to see if they slow down.

23. Specify that your drive-through order is "to go."

Computerized Diagnosis

One day, Pete complained to his friend, "My elbow really hurts. I guess I should see a doctor." His friend said, "Don't do that. There's a computer at the drug store that can diagnose anything quicker and cheaper than a doctor. Simply put in a sample of your urine, and the computer will diagnose your problem and tell you what you can do about it. And, it only costs $10.00." Pete figured he had nothing to lose, so he filled a jar with a urine sample and went to the drugstore. Finding the computer, he poured in the sample and deposited the $10.00. The computer started making some noise and various lights started flashing. After a brief pause, out popped a small slip of paper which read: you have tennis elbow. Soak your arm in warm water, avoid heavy labor. It will be better in two weeks.

That evening while thinking how amazing this new technology was and how it would change medical science forever, he began to wonder if this computer could be fooled. He decided to put it to the test. He mixed together some tap water, a stool sample from his dog, and urine samples from his wife and daughter. To top it off, he masturbated into the concoction. He went back to the drug store, located the computer, poured in the sample and deposited the $10.00. The machine again made the usual noises, flashed its lights, and printed out the following analysis:

Your tap water is too hard. Get a water softener.

Your dog has ringworm. Bathe him with anti-fungal shampoo.

Your daughter is using cocaine. Put her in a rehabilitation clinic.

Your wife is pregnant...... twin girls. They aren't yours. Get a lawyer.

And, if you don't stop jerking off, your elbow will never get better.

<u>Air Sick</u>

A little guy gets on a plane and sits next to the window. A few minutes later, a big, heavy, strong, mean-looking, hulking guy plops down in the seat next to him. The huge man glares threateningly at his neighbor, crowds the little guy so much that he's flattened against the window, and immediately falls asleep. After the plane takes off, the little guy starts to feel a little air sick, but he's afraid to wake the big guy up to ask if he can go to the bathroom. After a few attempts, he realizes that he can't climb over him, and so the little guy is sitting there, looking at the big guy, trying to decide what to do. Suddenly, the plane hits an air pocket and an uncontrollable wave of nausea passes over the little fellow. He just can't hold it in any longer and finally pukes all over the big guy's chest. About five minutes later the big guy wakes up, looks down, and sees the vomit all over him. "So," the little guy says brightly, "are you feeling better now?"

<u>Miscellaneous</u>

What'd I Win?

Early one morning, a drunk stumbling home from a long busy bar evening toddles into a bar near his home. It was just opening. "Mornin'," says the bartender, as the drunk tumbles onto a stool. Upon seeing the state of his first client, he comments, "Say Buddy, why don't you just go home and sleep it off?" Respectfully, the drunk declines, asking, "Shay, howsabout sum beer o' the dog what bit me?" The bartender shakes his head offering, "Okay, a short one, but then you're off for home. Right?" "Shure, shure," responds the drunk downing the glass of beer. Looking around the room, the drunk spots the dart board. "HEY, HEY, Hey, yous guys play darts? Lemme play!" The bartender says, "Okay, one dart and you leave." "Shure, shure," the drunk says as he flips the dart and almost falls to the floor. The dart hits the Bulls eye! "Hey hey hey, a bull's eye, whaddu I win?" Not knowing what to do, but wanting to get rid of the drunk, the bartender came up with an idea. He had found a box turtle on the way into work that day and had put it into a shoe box to take home to his son that night. Pulling out the box from under the bar, he handed it to the drunk. "Congratulations, now go home, Okay?" "Tanks," responded the drunk as he left, box clutched tightly under his arm.

Two weeks later. Same time of morning. Same bar. Same bartender. Same drunk. "Shay, 'member me?" "No," says the bartender setting out glasses for the day's business. "I t'rew da darts. I won da prize. Kin I t'row again?" "Oh yeah, Okay. But, then you're going home, right?" "Shure, shure," says the drunk as he gingerly takes the dart and heaves it at the board. Another Bull's Eye! "Hey hey hey, a bull's eye, whaddu I win?" "I don't know. What did I give you last time?" His eyes wide, the drunk says, "NO, NO!! Don't give me that. It was roast beef on a hard roll an' it was AWFUL!"

Excerpt From Court Transcripts

In a jury trial by his peers in Battleford, Sask., a farmer was charged with bestiality after he became amorous with one of his cows. The chief Crown witness, the hired man, testified that he saw his boss place a milk stool behind the cow, then stand on the stool and take liberties with the cow. Moments later, the witness said, the cow kicked over the stool and the farmer fell to the floor of the barn. Upon hearing this, a farmer in the jury box slapped his thigh and exclaimed, "They'll do that every time!"

The US Naval Ship

This is the transcript of an ACTUAL radio conversation of a US naval ship with Canadian authorities off the coast of Newfoundland in October, 1995. Radio conversation released by the Chief of Naval Operations 10-10-95.

Americans: Please divert your course 15 degrees to the North to avoid a collision.

Canadians: Recommend you divert YOUR course 15 degrees to the South to avoid a collision.

Americans: This is the Captain of a US Navy ship. I say again, divert YOUR course.

Canadians: No. I say again, you divert YOUR course.

Americans: THIS IS THE AIRCRAFT CARRIER USS LINCOLN, THE SECOND LARGEST SHIP IN THE UNITED STATES' ATLANTIC FLEET. WE ARE ACCOMPANIED BY THREE DESTROYERS, THREE CRUISERS AND NUMEROUS SUPPORT VESSELS. I DEMAND THAT YOU CHANGE YOUR COURSE 15 DEGREES NORTH, THAT'S ONE FIVE DEGREES NORTH, OR COUNTER-MEASURES WILL BE UNDERTAKEN TO ENSURE THE SAFETY OF THIS SHIP.

Canadians: This is a lighthouse. Your call.

The 10th Floor Winds

Two men are sitting drinking at a bar at the top of the Empire State Building when the first man turns to the other and says, "You know, last week I discovered that if you jump from the top of this building, by the time you fall to the 10th floor, the winds around the building are so intense that they carry you around the building and back into the window." The bartender just shakes his head in disapproval while wiping the bar. The second guy says, "What are you? A nut? There is no way in the world that could happen." "No, it's true," said the first man," let me prove it to you." He gets up from the bar, jumps over the balcony, and plummets toward the street below. When he passes the 10th floor, the high wind whips him around the building and back into the 10th floor window and he takes the elevator back up to the bar.

He met the second man, who looked quite astonished. "You know, I saw that with my own eyes, but that must have been a one time fluke." "No, I'll prove it again," says the fist man as he jumps. Again, just as he is hurling toward the street, the 10th floor wind gently carries him around the building and into the window. Once upstairs, he urges his fellow drinker to try it. "Well, what the heck," the second guy says, "it works, I'll try it!" He jumps over the balcony, plunges downward, passes the 11th, 10th, 9th, 8th floors ...and hits the sidewalk with a 'splat.' Back upstairs the Bartender turns to the other drinker, saying, "You know, you sure are a mean drunk Superman!"

1997 Ferrari GTO

A hip young man goes out and buys a 1997 Ferrari GTO. It is the best and most expensive car available in the world, costing about $500,000. He takes it out for a spin and while stopping for a red light, an old man on a Moped (both looking about 90 yrs old) pulls up next to him. The old man looks over the sleek, shiny surface of the car and asks, "What kind of a car ya' got there, sonny?" The young man replies, "A 1997 Ferrari GTO. They cost about a half million dollars!" "That's a lot of money," says the old man, shocked. "Why does it cost so much?" "Because this car can do up to 320 mph!," stated the cool dude proudly. The Moped driver asks, "Can I take a look inside?" "Sure," replies the owner. So, the old man pokes his head in the window and looks around. Leaning back on his Moped, he says, "That's a pretty nice car, all right!"

Just then, the light changes so the guy decides to show the old man what his car can do. He floors it, and within 30 seconds the speedometer reads 320 mph. Suddenly he notices a dot in his rear view mirror. It seems to be getting closer! He slows down to see what it could be and suddenly, Whhhooossshhh! Something whips by him, going much faster! "What on earth could be going faster than my Ferrari?!" the young man asks himself. Then, ahead of him, he sees a dot coming toward him. Whoooossshh! It goes by again, heading the opposite direction! It looks almost like the old man on the Moped. "Couldn't be," thinks the guy. "How could a Moped outrun a Ferrari?!" Again, he sees a dot in his rear view mirror. Whoosshh! Ka-BbllaaMMM! It plows into the back of his car, demolishing the rear end. The young man jumps out, and it IS the old man!!! Of course, the Moped and the old man are hurting. He runs up to the old man and says, "You're hurt! Is there anything I can do for you?" The old man moans and replies, "Yes....unhook my suspenders from your side-view mirror!"

Sit Back And Relax

A plane was taking off from Kennedy Airport. After it reached a comfortable cruising altitude, the captain made an announcement over the intercom, "Ladies and gentlemen, this is your captain speaking. Welcome to Flight Number 293, nonstop from New York to Los Angeles. The weather ahead is good and, therefore, we should have a smooth and uneventful flight. Now sit back and relax...OH MY GOD!" Silence followed and after a few minutes, the captain came back on the intercom and said, "Ladies and Gentlemen, I am so sorry if I scared you earlier, but while I was talking, the flight-attendant brought me a cup of coffee and spilled the hot coffee in my lap. You should see the front of my pants!" A passenger in coach said, "That's nothing. He should see the back of mine!"

Justice

Now here's a mouthful of Justice!! Deputy Sheriff Kevin Skurat of Bentonn Illinois was dispatched to a burglary call. When he arrived at the scene, he was met by the complaining party. It seems someone had broken into his large barn sometime during the night. He took the Deputy to the door and showed him where the perpetrator had pried his way into the building and they entered the building. They saw what appeared to be where someone had thrown up or had a bowel movement. Deputy Skurat made the observation that the perpetrator was probably intoxicated and had thrown-up. However, the complainant disagreed with him about this. He told the Deputy that he had another idea why the would-be thief had gotten sick. Inside this barn was a large motor home. Sitting on the floor, near the side of the vehicle was a five gallon gas can. Near the gas can was a piece of siphoning hose. It was obvious that the perpetrator had intended to steal some gas from the motor home. However, he had made an error in doing so.

Being unfamiliar with this type of vehicle, the perpetrator had removed the gas cap, or so he thought. He then stuck in the siphon hose, placed his mouth on the other end of the hose and began to suck. The only problem was the perpetrator had not taken off the gas cap, but had removed the cap that goes to the portable sewage container. The complainant advised Deputy Skurat that he had just gotten back from a camping trip and had not had a chance to empty the sewage tank. So, instead of drawing up gasoline from the tank, the perpetrator had drawn up of mouth full of raw human sewage.

Jet Fuel Drunks

A couple of drinking buddies who are airplane mechanics are in a hangar in Atlanta Airport; it's fogged in and they have nothing to do. One of them says to the other "Man, have you got anything to drink?" "Nah, but I hear you can drink jet fuel - that'll kinda give you a buzz." So they drink some jet fuel, get smashed and have a beautiful time; like only drinkin' buddies can. The following morning, one of them wakes up and he knows his head will explode if he gets up. But, it doesn't. He gets up and feels good; in fact, he feels great - NO hangover! The phone rings; it's his buddy. The buddy says "Hey, how do you feel?" He said, "I feel great!!" The other guy says, "I feel great, too!! You don't have a hangover?" The first guy says, "No. No hangover. That jet fuel is great stuff! We ought to do this more often." "Yeah, we could, but there's just one thing..." "What's that?" "Did you fart yet?" "What??" "Did you FART yet??" "No..." "Well, DON'T, 'cause I'm in Phoenix.

A Passion For Baked Beans

Once upon a time, there lived a woman who had a maddening passion for baked beans. She loved them but unfortunately they had, in typical fashion, always caused a somewhat lively and very embarrassing reaction. Then, one day she met a guy and fell in love. When it became apparent that they would marry, she thought to herself, "He is such a sweet and gentle man, he would never go for this carrying on." So she made the supreme sacrifice and gave up beans. Some months later, her car broke down on the way home from work. They lived in the country and she decided rather than bothering her husband, she would simply walk home. So, she called her husband and told him that she would be bit late. On her way, she passed a small diner and the odor of the baked beans was more than she could stand. Since she still had a couple of miles to walk, she figured that she would walk off any ill effects by the time she reached home. So, she stopped at the diner and before she knew it, she had consumed three large orders of baked beans.

All the way home she putt-putted. And, upon arriving home she felt reasonably sure she could control any further reactions. As she walked in the front door, her husband seemed excited to see her and exclaimed delightedly, "Darling, I have a surprise for dinner tonight." He then blindfolded her and led her to her chair at the table. She seated herself and just as he was about to remove the blindfold from his wife, the telephone rang. He made her promise not to touch the blindfold until he returned. He then went to answer the phone. The baked beans she had consumed were still affecting her and the pressure was becoming almost unbearable. So, while her husband was out of the room she seized the opportunity, shifted her weight to one cheek, and let it go. It was not only loud, but it smelled like cabbage cooking in a high school locker room on a hot August afternoon. She found her napkin and fanned the air around her vigorously. Then, she shifted to the other cheek and ripped three more. At this point, it smelled like a bulk truck full of rotten potatoes running over a skunk in front of the pulpwood mill in Lincoln.

When the phone farewells signaled the end of her freedom, she fanned the air a few more times with her napkin, placed it on her lap and folded her hands upon it, smiling contentedly to herself. She was the picture of innocence when her husband returned. Apologizing for taking so long, he asked her if she peeked, and she assured him that she had not. At this point, he removed the blindfold, and there was her surprise!!! Twelve dinner guests seated around the table to wish her a Happy Birthday!!!

Beethoven's Grave

A tourist in Vienna is going through a graveyard and all of a sudden he hears some music. No one is around, so he starts searching for the source. He finally locates the origin and finds it is coming from a grave with a headstone that reads: Ludwig van Beethoven, 1770-1827. Then, he realizes that the music is the Ninth Symphony and it is being played backward! Puzzled, he leaves the graveyard and persuades a friend to return with him. By the time they arrive back at the grave, the music has changed. This time it is the Seventh Symphony, but like the previous piece, it is being played backward. Curious, the men agree to consult a music scholar. When they return with the expert, the Fifth Symphony is playing, again backward. The expert notices that the symphonies are being played in the reverse order in which they were composed, the 9th, then the 7th, then the 5th. By the next day, the word has spread and a throng has gathered around the grave. They are all listening to the Second Symphony being played backward. Just then, the graveyard's caretaker ambles up to the group. Someone in the group asks him if he has an explanation for the music. "Don't you get it?" the caretaker says incredulously. [Guess now, before scrolling down]

No cheating, make a guess before scrolling

not even a wild guess before scrolling?

He's de-composing!

The Employee Evaluation

THE BOSS ASKED FOR A LETTER DESCRIBING BOB SMITH:
Bob Smith, my assistant programmer, can always be found
hard at work in his cubicle. Bob works independently, without
wasting company time talking to colleagues. Bob never
thinks twice about assisting fellow employees, and he always
finishes given assignments on time. Often, Bob takes extended
measures to complete his work, sometimes skipping coffee
breaks. Bob is a dedicated individual who has absolutely no
vanity in spite of his high accomplishments and profound
knowledge in his field. I firmly believe that Bob can be
classed as a high-caliber employee, the type which cannot be
dispensed with. Consequently, I duly recommend that Bob be
promoted to executive management, and a proposal will be
executed as soon as possible.
Sd/-
Project Leader

A MEMO WAS SOON SENT FOLLOWING THE LETTER:
   The employee was reading over my shoulder while I wrote the report sent to
you earlier. Kindly read only the odd numbered lines (1, 3, 5, etc...) for my true
assessment of him. Regards.

A Genie And 3 Guys

   Three guys, an Iowan, a Wisconsinite, and a Minnesotan are out walking
along the beach together one day. They come across a lantern and a Genie pops out
of it. "I will give you each one wish, that's three wishes total," says the Genie. The
Iowan says, "I am a farmer, my dad was a farmer, and my son will also farm. I want
the land to be forever fertile in Iowa." With a blink of the Genie's eye, FOOM...the
land in Iowa was forever made fertile for farming. The Wisconsinite was amazed, so
he said, "I want a wall around Wisconsin, so that no one can come into our precious
state." Again, with a blink of the Genie's eye, POOF there was a huge wall around
Wisconsin. The Minnesotan asks, "I'm very curious. Please tell me more about this
wall." The Genie explains, "Well, it's about 150 feet high, 50 feet thick and nothing
can get in or out." The Minnesotan says, "Fill it up with water."

A Genie In California

A man was walking along a California beach when he stumbled across an old lamp. He picked it up and rubbed it and out popped a genie. The genie said, "OK, so you released me from the lamp blah blah blah, but this is the fourth time this week and I'm getting a little sick of these wishes, so you can forget about three. You only get one wish." The man sat and thought about it for a while and said, "I've always wanted to go to Hawaii but I'm too scared to fly and I get very seasick. So, could you build me a bridge to Hawaii so I can drive over there?" The genie laughed a replied, "That's impossible. Think of the logistics of that. How would the supports ever reach the bottom of the Pacific? Think of how much concrete... How much steel!!! No, think of another wish." The man agreed and tried to think of a really good wish. He said, "I've been married and divorced four times. My wives have always said I don't care and that I'm insensitive. I wish that I could understand women. To know what they are thinking when they give me the silent treatment, to know why they are crying, to know what they want when they say "nothing"... The genie replies, "So, you want that bridge two lanes or four?"

The DUI

One night, a police officer was staking out a particularly rowdy bar for possible violations of driving-under-the-influence laws. At closing time, he saw a fellow stumble out of the bar, trip on the curb, and try his keys on five different cars before he found his own car. Then, he sat in the front seat fumbling with his keys for several minutes. During this time, everyone left the bar and drove off. Finally, the fellow started his engine and began to pull away. The police officer was waiting for him. He stopped the driver, read him his rights and administered the breath test. The results showed a reading of 0.0. The puzzled officer demanded to know how that could be. The driver explained, "Tonight, I'm the designated decoy."

Hokey Pokey

I usually don't pass on news like this. I know you are all busy, but sometimes we have to pause and truly remember what life is all about. So, I pass on this sad, sad news....There was a great loss today in the entertainment world. The man who wrote the song, "Hokey Pokey" died. What was really horrible is that they had trouble keeping the body in the casket. They'd put his left leg in and....well, you know the rest.

The Nova Awards

These are the nominees for the Chevy Nova Award. This is given out in Honor of the GM's fiasco in trying to market this car in Central and South America. "No va" means, of course, in Spanish, "it doesn't go."

1. The Dairy Association's huge success with the campaign "Got Milk?" prompted them to expand advertising to Mexico. It was soon brought to their attention the Spanish translation read "Are you lactating?"

2. Coors put its slogan, "Turn It Loose," into Spanish, where it was read as "Suffer From Diarrhea."

3. Scandinavian vacuum manufacturer Electrolux used the following in an American campaign: "Nothing sucks like an Electrolux"

4. Clairol introduced the "Mist Stick," a curling iron, into Germany only to find out that "mist" is slang for manure.

5. When Gerber started selling baby food in Africa, they used the same packaging as in the US, with the smiling baby on the label. Later they learned that in Africa, companies routinely put pictures on the labels of what's inside, since many people can't read.

6. Colgate introduced a toothpaste in France called Cue, the name of a notorious porno magazine.

7. An American T-shirt maker in Miami printed shirts for the Spanish market which promoted the Pope's visit. Instead of "I Saw the Pope" (el Papa), the shirts read "I Saw the Potato" (la papa).

8. Pepsi's "Come Alive With the Pepsi Generation" translated into "Pepsi Brings Your Ancestors Back From the Grave" in Chinese.

9. The Coca-Cola name in China was first read as "Kekoukela," meaning "Bite the wax tadpole" or "female horse stuffed with wax," depending on the dialect. Coke then researched 40,000 characters to find a phonetic equivalent "kokou kole," translating into "happiness in the mouth."

10. Frank Perdue's chicken slogan, "It takes a strong man to make a tender chicken" was translated into Spanish as "it takes an aroused man to make a chicken affectionate."

11. When Parker Pen marketed a ball-point pen in Mexico, its ads were supposed to have read, "It won't leak in your pocket and embarrass you." The company thought that the word "embarazar" (to impregnate) meant to embarrass, so the ad read: "It won't leak in your pocket and make you pregnant!"

12. When American Airlines wanted to advertise its new leather first class seats in the Mexican market, it translated its "Fly In Leather" campaign literally, which meant "Fly Naked" (vuela en cuero) in Spanish.

The Irate Customer

An award should go to the United Airlines gate agent in Denver for being smart, funny, and making her point when confronted with a passenger who probably deserved to fly as cargo. A crowded flight was canceled. A single agent was rebooking a long line of inconvenienced travelers. Suddenly, an angry passenger pushed his way to the desk. He slapped his ticket down on the counter and said, "I HAVE to be on this flight and it has to be FIRST CLASS." The agent replied, "I'm sorry sir. I'll be happy to try to help you but I've got to help these folks first, and I'm sure we'll be able to work something out." The passenger was unimpressed. He asked loudly, so that the passengers behind him could hear, "Do you have any idea who I am?" Without hesitating, the gate agent smiled and grabbed her public address microphone. "May I have your attention please?" she began, her voice bellowing throughout the terminal. "We have a passenger here at the gate WHO DOES NOT KNOW WHO HE IS. If anyone can help him find his identity, please come to the gate." With the folks behind him in line laughing hysterically, the man glared at the United agent, gritted his teeth and swore, "F*** YOU." Without flinching, she smiled and said, "I'm sorry, sir, but you'll have to stand in line for that, too."

J.D. Heskin

Assorted Jokes

What do Eskimos get from sitting on the ice too long?
Polaroids.

What do prisoners use to call each other?
Cell phones.

What kind of coffee was served on the Titanic?
Sanka.

How do crazy people go through the forest?
They take the psycho path.

What does it mean when the flag is at half-mast at the post office?
They're hiring.

How do you get holy water?
Boil the hell out of it.

What did the fish say when it hit a concrete wall?
"Dam!"

What do you call a boomerang that doesn't work?
A stick.

What do you call cheese that isn't yours?
Nacho Cheese.

What do you call Santa's helpers?
Subordinate Clauses.

What do you call four bullfighters in quicksand?
Quatro sinko.

What do you get from a pampered cow?
Spoiled milk.

What do you get when you cross a snowman with a vampire?
Frostbite.

What has four legs, is big, green, fuzzy, and would kill you if it fell out of a tree?
A pool table.

What lies at the bottom of the ocean and twitches?
A nervous wreck.

What's the difference between roast beef and pea soup?
Anyone can roast beef.

Where do you find a dog with no legs?
Right where you left him.

Why do bagpipers walk when they play?
They're trying to get away from the noise.

Why do gorillas have big nostrils?
Because they have big fingers.

What's the difference between an oral thermometer and a rectal thermometer?
The taste.

What is a zebra?
An undergarment that's 25 sizes larger than an "A" bra.

Did you hear about the flasher that was thinking about retiring?
He decided to stick it out for one more year.

What do you get when you cross a pit bull with a collie?
A dog that runs for help after it bites your leg off.

What's the difference between a quickee and a Yankee?
A quickee involves two people while a Yankee involves one.

How do you get 500 cows into a barn?
Put up a "Bingo" sign.

What do the letters D.N.A stand for?
National Dyslexia Association.

Why are there so many Smiths in the phone book?
They all have phones.

Two flies feasting...
Two flies are feasting on a piece of dog crap when one fly rips off a huge fart. The other fly looks at him and says, "Hey, I'm trying to eat here."

Vocabulary Builders

1. AQUADEXTROUS (ak wa deks' trus) adj. Possessing the ability to turn the bathtub faucet on and off with your toes.

2. CARPERPETUATION (kar' pur pet u a shun) n. The act, when vacuuming, of running over a string or a piece of lint at least a dozen times, reaching over and picking it up, examining it, then putting it back down to give the vacuum one more chance.

3. DISCONFECT (dis kon fekt') v. To sterilize the piece of candy you dropped on the floor by blowing on it, assuming this will somehow 'remove' all the germs.

4. ELBONICS (el bon' iks) n. The actions of two people maneuvering for one armrest in a movie theater (airplane).

5. FRUST (frust) n. The small line of debris that refuses to be swept onto the dust pan and keep backing a person across the room until he finally decides to give up and sweep it under the rug.

6. LACTOMANGULATION (lak' to man guy lay' shun) n. Manhandling the "open here" spout on a milk container so badly that one has to resort to the 'illegal' side.

7. PEPPIER (pehp ee ay') n. The waiter at a fancy restaurant whose sole purpose seems to be walking around asking diners if they want ground pepper.

8. PHONESIA (fo nee' zhuh) n. The affliction of dialing a phone number and forgetting whom you were calling just as they answer.

9. PUPKUS (pup'kus) n. The moist residue left on a window after a dog presses its nose to it.

10. TELECRASTINATION (tel e kras tin ay' shun) n. The act of always letting the phone ring at least twice before you pick it up, even when you're only six inches away.

Minnesota Driving Rules

A right lane closure is just a game to see how many people can cut in line by passing you on the right as you sit in the left lane waiting for the same jerks to squeeze their way back in before hitting the orange construction barrels.

Turn signals give away your next move. A real Minneapolis driver never uses them.

Under no circumstances should you leave a safe distance between you and the car in front of you, or the space will be filled in by somebody else, putting you in an even more dangerous situation.

Crossing two or more lanes in a single lane-change is considered "going with the flow."

The faster you drive through a red light, the smaller chance you have of getting hit.

Braking is to be done as hard and as late as possible to ensure that your ABS kicks in, giving a nice, relaxing foot massage as the brake pedal pulsates. For those without ABS, it's a chance to stretch your legs.

The new electronic traffic warning signs are not there to provide useful information. They are only there to make Minnesota look high-tech and to distract you from seeing the highway patrol car parked in the median.

Never pass on the left when you can pass on the right. It's a good way to scare people entering the highway.

Speed limits are arbitrary figures, given only as suggestions and are apparently not enforceable in the metro area during rush hour.

Just because you're in the left lane and have no room to speed up or move over doesn't mean that a Minneapolis driver, flashing his high beams behind you, doesn't think he can go faster in your spot.

Please remember that there is no such thing as a shortcut during rush-hour traffic in Minneapolis.

Always slow down and rubberneck when you see an accident, or even someone changing a tire.

Throwing litter on the road adds variety to the landscape, keeps the existing litter from getting lonely, and gives Adopt-a-Highway crews something to clean up.

Everybody thinks their vehicle is better than yours, especially those in pickup trucks with stickers of Calvin peeing on a Ford, Dodge, or Chevy logo.

Learn to swerve abruptly. Minnesota is the home of high-speed slalom driving thanks to our city councils, who put potholes in key locations to test drivers' reflexes and keep them on their toes.

It is traditional in the Twin Cities to honk your horn at cars that don't move the instant the light changes.

Seeking eye contact with another driver revokes your right of way.

Remember that the goal of every Minnesota driver is to get there first, by whatever means necessary.

Real Minnesota women drivers can put on pantyhose and apply eye makeup at seventy-five miles per hour in bumper-to-bumper traffic.

All Minnesota drivers are required to use a cellular phone while driving. It makes it easier to call 911 when they hit someone and the Minnesota Highway Patrol can respond more quickly to block off two or more lanes or traffic... Especially during rush hour.

Heavy fog, rain, and snow are not reasons to change any of the previously listed rules. These weather conditions are God's way of ensuring the economic well-being of body-shops, junk yards, and new vehicle sales.

How To Stop Telemarketers

1. If they want to loan you money, tell them you just filed for bankruptcy and you could sure use some money. Ask, "How long can I keep it? Do I have to ever pay it back, or is it like the other money I borrowed before my bankruptcy?"

2. If you get one of those pushy people who won't shut up, just listen to their sales pitch. When they try to close the sale, tell them that you'll need to go get your credit card. Then, just set the phone down and go do laundry, shopping or whatever. See how long that commission based scum waits for you to get your credit card.

3. If they start out with, "How are you today?" say, "Why do you want to know?" Or you can say, "I'm so glad you asked, because no one seems to care these days and I have all these problems, my sciatica is acting up, my eyelashes are sore, my dog just died...." When they try to get back to the sales process, just continue on with telling about your problems.

4. If the person says he's Joe Doe from the ABC Company, ask him to spell his name, then ask him to spell the company name, then ask where it is located. Continue asking personal questions or questions about the company for as long as necessary.

5. This one works better if you are male: Telemarketer: "Hi, my name is Julie and I'm with Dodger & Peck Services.... You: "Hang on a second." (few seconds pause) "Okay, (in a really husky voice) what are you wearing?"

6. Crying out, in well-simulated tones of pleasure and surprise, "Julie! Is this really you? I can't believe it! Julie, how have you BEEN?" Hopefully, this will give Julie a few brief moments of terror as she tries to figure out where the heck she could know you from.

7. Say, "No," over and over. Be sure to vary the sound of each no, and keep an even tempo even as they're trying to speak. This is the most fun if you can keep going until they hang up.

8. If MCI calls trying to get you to sign up with their Family and Friends plan, reply, in as sinister a voice as you can muster, "I don't have any friends...would you be my friend?"

9. If they clean rugs: "Can you get blood out, you can? Well, how about goat blood or HUMAN blood - chicken blood too?"

10. Let the person go through their spiel, providing minimal but necessary feedback in the form of an occasional "Uh-huh, really, or, "That's fascinating." Finally, when they ask you to buy, ask them to marry you. They get all flustered, but just tell them you couldn't give your credit card number to someone who's a complete stranger.

11. Tell them you work for the same company they work for. Example:
Telemarketer: "This is Bill from Widget & Associates."
You: "Widget & Associates! Hey I work for them too. Where are you calling from?"
Telemarketer: "Uh, Dallas, Texas."
You: "Great, they have a group there too? How's business/the weather? Too bad the company has a policy against selling to employees! Oh well, see ya."

12. Tell the Telemarketer you are busy and if they will give you their phone number you will call them back. If they say they are not allowed to give out their number, then ask them for their home number and tell them you will call them at home (this is usually the most effective method of getting rid of Telemarketers). If the person says, "Well, I don't really want to get a call at home," say, "Ya! Now you know how I feel." (smiling, of course...)

13. My personal favorite way to Make a Telemarketer Go Away involves the help of my 3 year old son. When they call and ask to speak with Mr. Stevens, I explain they want the "other Mr. Stevens." As I hand the phone to my son, I tell him to explain all the fun things he did that day, from the detailed slimy booger he picked and where he wiped it, to his favorite and most proud stories about "pooping in the toilet." He is so proud of the shapes he can make. Usually after a few minutes of running around on the cordless phone explaining how proud he was with the details of his day, he comes back and says "they hung up." Imagine the rudeness of some people.....Go figure....

How To Argue Effectively

I argue very well. Ask any of my remaining friends. I can win an argument on any topic, against any opponent. People know this and steer clear of me at parties. Often, as a sign of their great respect, they don't even invite me. You too can win arguments. Simply follow these rules:

*Drink liquor.

Suppose you are at a party and some hotshot intellectual is expounding on the economy of Peru, a subject you know nothing about. If you're drinking some health-fanatic drink like grapefruit juice, you'll hang back, afraid to display your ignorance, while the hotshot enthralls your date. But, if you drink several large cocktails, you'll discover you have STRONG VIEWS about the Peruvian economy. You'll be a WEALTH of information. You'll argue forcefully, offering searing insights and possibly upsetting furniture. People will be impressed. Some may even leave the room.

*Make things up.

Suppose, in the Peruvian economy argument, you are trying to prove that Peruvians are underpaid, a position you base solely on the fact that YOU are underpaid, and you'll be damned if you're going to let a bunch of Peruvians be better off. DON'T say, "I think Peruvians are underpaid." Say instead, "The average Peruvian's salary in 2013 dollars adjusted for the revised tax base is $1,452.81 per annum, which is $836.07 before the mean gross poverty level."

NOTE: Always make up exact figures.

If an opponent asks you where you got your information, make THAT up too. Say, "This information comes from Dr. Hovel T. Moon's study for the Buford Commission published on May 9, 2013. Didn't you read it?" Say this in the same tone of voice you would use to say, "You left your soiled underwear in my bathroom."

*Use meaningless but weighty-sounding words and phrases.
Memorize this list:
>Let me put it this way
>In terms of
>Vis-à-vis
>Per se
>As it were
>Qua
>So to speak

You should also memorize some Latin abbreviations such as "QED," "e.g.," and "i.e." These are all short for "I speak Latin, and you don't."

How To Argue Effectively, continued

Here's how to use these words and phrases. Suppose you want to say, "Peruvians would like to order appetizers more often, but they don't have enough money." You never win arguments talking like that. But, you WILL win if you say, "Let me put it this way. In terms of appetizers vis-à-vis Peruvians qua Peruvians, they would like to order them more often, so to speak, but they do not have enough money per se, as it were. QED." Only a fool would challenge that statement.

*Use snappy and irrelevant comebacks.

You need an arsenal of all-purpose irrelevant phrases to fire back at your opponents when they make valid points. The best are:

You're begging the question.
You're being defensive.
Don't compare apples to oranges.
What are your parameters?

This last one is especially valuable. Nobody (other than psychometricians and policy wonks) has the vaguest idea what "parameters" means.

Don't forget the classic: YOU'RE SO LINEAR!

Here's how to use your comebacks:

You say: As Abraham Lincoln said in 1873...
Your opponent says: Lincoln died in 1865.
You say: You're begging the question.

You say: Liberians, like most Asians...
Your opponent says: Liberia is in Africa.
You say: You're being defensive.

*Compare your opponent to Adolf Hitler.

This is your heavy artillery, for when your opponent is obviously right and you are spectacularly wrong. Bring Hitler up subtly. Say, "That sounds suspiciously like something Adolf Hitler might say," or "You certainly do remind me of Adolf Hitler."

Ole, Lars and Sven

Ole, Lars and Sven had been going to the Sons Of Norway hall meeting as long as there had been a hall. And every month, wouldn't ya know it, they didn't win a prize in the monthly drawing. That is until last month's meeting. Sven was the first one of the three to get his name drawn. He won two pounds of spaghetti sauce, four boxes of noodles, and three pounds of (Swedish) meatballs. Ole had his name drawn next. He got himself round trip tickets to Duluth, a night's stay at the Dew Drop Inn and a pair of tickets to see the Inger Triplets polka ensemble. Ole thought that he had died and gone to heaven. Lars was the last one to have his name drawn, he won a toilet brush. At the next monthly meeting, they sat down together to check out how they had fared for the past month. Sven said, "Uff da, I had dat pasghetti for tree days. It was so good, and Helga didn't have to buy food for them dere tree days." Ole said, "Lena was so happy vhen I brought home dem tickets. The trip up to Duloot was nice, we got to ride da Greyhound, and you know, they got a built-in outhouse on dat dere bus. And the Inger Triplets, if I didn't know better, I would swear dey were sisters." Then, Ole turned to Lars, and asked him how his prize worked out. Lars looks at them both and says, "Dat dere toilet brush is nice, but I tink I'll go back to using paper."

Actual News Headlines
(Compiled by the Columbia School of Journalism)

1. Something Went Wrong in Jet Crash, Expert Says
2. Police Begin Campaign to Run Down Jaywalkers
3. Safety Experts Say School Bus Passengers Should Be Belted
4. Drunk Gets Nine Months in Violin Case
5. Survivor of Siamese Twins Joins Parents
6. Farmer Bill Dies in House
7. Iraqi Head Seeks Arms
8. Is There a Ring of Debris Around Uranus
9. Stud Tires Out
10. Prostitutes Appeal to Pope
11. Panda Mating Fails, Veterinarian Takes Over
12. Soviet Virgin Lands Short of Goal Again
13. British Left Waffles on Falkland Islands
14. Lung Cancer in Women Mushrooms
15. Eye Drops off Shelf
16. Teacher Strikes Idle Kids
17. Reagan Wins on Budget, but More Lies Ahead
18. Squad Helps Dog Bite Victim
19. Enraged Cow Injures Farmer with Ax
21. Plane Too Close to Ground, Crash Probe Told
22. Miners Refuse to Work After Death
23. Juvenile Court to Try Shooting Defendant
24. Stolen Painting Found by Tree

25. Two Soviet Ships Collide, One Dies
26. Two Sisters Reunited After 18 Years in Checkout Counter
27. Killer Sentenced to Die for Second Time in Ten Years
28. Never Withhold Herpes Infection from Loved One
29. Drunken Driver Pays $1000 in '84
30. War Dims Hope for Peace
31. If Strike Isn't Settled Quickly, It May Last a While
32. Cold Wave Linked to Temperature
33. Enfields Couple Slain: Police Suspect Homicide
34. Red Tape Holds Up New Bridge
35. Deer Kill 17,000
36. Typhoon Rips Through Cemetery; Hundreds Dead
37. Man Struck by Lightning Faces Battery Charges
38. New Study of Obesity Looks for Larger Test Group
39. Astronaut Takes Blame for gas in Spacecraft
40. Kids Make Nutritious Snacks
41. Chef Throws His Heart Into Helping the Needy
42. Arson Suspect is Geld in Massachusetts Fire
43. British Union Finds Dwarfs in Short Supply
44. Ban on Soliciting dead in Trotwood
45. Lansing Residents Can Drop Off Trees
46. Local High School Dropouts Cut in Half
47. New Vaccine May Contain Rabies
48. Man Minus ear Waives Hearing
49. Deaf College Opens Doors to Hearing
50. Air Head Fired
51. Man Steals Clock, Faces Time
52. Prosecutor Releases Probe Into Undersheriff
53. Old School Pillars are Replaced by Alumni
54. Bank Drive-In Window Blocked by Board
55. Hospitals are Sued by 7 Foot Doctors
56. Some Pieces of Rock Hudson Sold at Auction
57. Sex Education Delayed, Teachers Request Training
58. Include Your Children When Baking Cookies

How To Tell You're In Southern California

Your co-worker tells you he/she has 8 body piercings.....and none are visible.

You make over $250,000 and still can't afford a house.

An earthquake rumbles through at 2AM and, if it wakes you up at all, you lay in bed, guess the magnitude and duration, and then decide if it's worth while to get up.

Your child's 3rd grade teacher has purple hair, a nose ring and is named Breeze.

You can't remember.....is pot illegal?

You've been to more than one baby shower that has two mothers and a sperm donor.

A really great parking space can move you to tears.

A low-speed police pursuit will interrupt ANY TV broadcast.

You're thinking of taking an adult class but you can't decide between aromatherapy and conversational Mandarin.

Gas costs 50 cents a gallon more than anywhere else in the United States.

A man walks on the bus in full leather regalia and crotchless chaps. You don't notice. A woman walks on the bus with live poultry. You don't notice.

Unlike back home, the guy at 8:30 a.m. at Starbucks wearing the baseball cap and sunglasses who looks like George Clooney IS George Clooney.

Your car insurance costs as much as your house payment.

Your hairdresser is straight, your plumber is gay, the woman who delivers your mail is into BDSM and your Mary Kay Cosmetic Lady is a guy in drag.

You call 911 and they put you on hold.

You have to leave the big company meeting early because Billy Blanks himself is teaching the 4:30 Tae-bo class.

Your paper boy has a two picture deal.

The three hour traffic jam you just sat through wasn't caused by a horrific 9 car pile-up but by everyone slowing to rubberneck at a lost shoe laying on the shoulder.

Idiots Everywhere

IDIOTS AT WORK:
Sign in a gas station: Coke -- 49 cents each. Two for a dollar.

IDIOTS AT WORK 2:
I was signing the receipt for my credit card purchase when the clerk noticed that I had never signed my name on the back of the credit card. She informed me that she could not complete the transaction unless the card was signed. When asked why, she explained that it was necessary to compare the signature on the credit card with the signature I just signed on the receipt. So, I signed the credit card in front of her. She carefully compared that signature to the one I signed on the receipt. As luck would have it, they matched.

IDIOTS IN THE NEIGHBORHOOD:
I live in a semi rural area. We recently had a new neighbor call the local township administrative office to request the removal of the Deer Crossing sign on our road. The reason: Many deer were being hit by cars and he no longer wanted them to cross there.

IDIOTS AND COMPUTERS:
My neighbor works in the operations department in the central office of a large bank. Employees in the field call him when they have problems with their computers. One night he got a call from a woman in one of the branch banks who had this question, "I've got smoke coming from the back of my terminal. Do you guys have a fire downtown?"

IDIOTS ARE EASY TO PLEASE:
I was sitting in my science class, when the teacher commented that the next day would be the shortest day of the year. My lab partner became visibly excited, cheering and clapping. I explained to her that the amount of daylight changes, not the actual amount of time. Needless to say, she was very disappointed.

IDIOTS IN FOOD SERVICE:
My daughter went to a local Taco Bell and ordered a taco. She asked the individual behind the counter for "minimal lettuce." He said he was sorry, but they only had iceberg.

Dear Diary

May 30th -- Now Texas is a state that knows how to live! Beautiful sunny days and warm balmy evenings. Mountains and deserts blended together. What a place! Watched the sunset from a park lying on a blanket. It was beautiful. I've finally found my home I love it here.

June 14th -- Really heating up. Got to 100 today. Not a problem. Live in an air-conditioned home, drive an air-conditioned car. What a pleasure to see the sun every day like this. I'm turning into a real sun worshipper.

June 30th -- Had the backyard landscaped with western plants today. Lots of cactus and rocks. What a breeze to maintain. No more mowing for me. Another scorcher today, but I love it here.

July 10th -- The temperature hasn't been below 100 all week. How do people get used to this kind of heat? At least it's a dry heat. Getting used to it is taking longer than I expected.

July 15th -- Fell asleep by the pool. (Got 3rd degree burns over 60% of my body.) Missed two days of work, what a dumb thing to do. I learned my lesson though: got to respect the ol' sun in a climate like this.

July 20th -- I missed Tabby (our cat) sneaking into the car when I left this morning. By the time I got out to the hot car for lunch, Tabby had swollen up to the size of a shopping bag and exploded all over $2,000 worth of leather upholstery. I told the kids she ran away. The car now smells like Kibbles and shit. No more pets in this heat!

July 25th -- Dry heat, my butt. Hot is hot!! The air-conditioner is on the fritz and AC repairman charged $200 just to drive by and tell me he needed to order parts.

July 30th -- Been sleeping outside by the pool for three nights now. $1,100 in damn house payments and we can't even go inside. Why did I ever come here?

Aug 4th -- 115 degrees. Finally got the air-conditioner fixed today. It cost $500 and gets the temperature down to about 90. Stupid repairman pissed in my pool. I hate this state.

Aug 8th -- If another wise ass cracks, "Hot enough for you today?", I'm going to tear his throat out. Damn heat. By the time I get to work the radiator is boiling over, my clothes are soaking wet, and I smell like roasted Garfield!!

Aug 10th -- The weather report might as well be a damn recording: Hot and Sunny. It's been too hot to for two damn months and the weatherman says it might really warm up next week. Doesn't it ever rain in this barren damn desert?? Water rationing has been in effect all summer, so $1,700 worth of cactus just dried up and blew into the pool. Even a cactus can't live in this heat.

Aug 14th -- Welcome to Hell!!! Temperature got to 123 today. Forgot to crack the window and blew the windshield out of the Lincoln. The installer came to fix it and said, "Hot enough for you today?" My wife had to spend the $1,100 house payment to bail me out of jail.

Aug 30th -- Worst day of the damn summer. I'm not leaving the house. The monsoon rains finally came and all they did is to make it muggier than hell. The Lincoln is now floating somewhere in Mexico with its new $500 windshield. That does it, we're moving to New York for some peace and quiet.

Politics

Clinton And The Pope

Clinton and the Pope are traveling together on Air Force One when the plane crashes and all aboard are killed. As the two ascend to the Pearly Gates, a freakish error occurs, and the Pope is sent straight to hell while Clinton enters heaven. Realizing the error within minutes, God sends an angel to hell to retrieve the Pontiff. "We're so sorry, your holiness," says the angel. "It was all a terrible mistake. God has given me the authority to grant you any one single wish in order to rectify this inconvenience." The Pope thinks on this during the trip up to heaven, and when they reach the Pearly Gates, he tells the angel, "I've always wanted to meet the Blessed Virgin Mary herself, so that's my one wish. The angel looks sheepish and says, "In that case, your holiness, we got you here just a few minutes too late."

Golf Frog

A man takes the day off work and decides to go out golfing. He is on the second hole when he notices a frog sitting next to the green. He thinks nothing of it and is about to shoot when he hears, "Ribbit, 9 Iron." The man looks around and doesn't see anyone. Again, he hears, "Ribbit, 9 Iron." He looks at the frog and decides to prove the frog wrong. He puts the club away, and grabs a 9 iron. Boom! He hits it 10 inches from the cup. He is shocked. He says to the frog, "Wow that's amazing. You must be a lucky frog, eh?" The frog replies, "Ribbit, Lucky frog." The man decides to take the frog with him to the next hole. "What do you think frog?," the man asks. "Ribbit, 3 wood." The guy takes out a 3 wood and, Boom! Hole in one. The man is befuddled and doesn't know what to say. By the end of the day, the man golfed the best game of golf in his life and asks the frog, "OK, where to next?" The frog replies, "Ribbit Las Vegas."

They go to Las Vegas and the guy says, "OK frog, now what?" The frog says, "Ribbit, Roulette." Upon approaching the roulette table, the man asks, "What do you think I should bet?" The frog replies, "Ribbit, $3000, black 6." Now, this is a thirty-five-to-one shot to win. But, after the golf game, the man figures what the heck. Boom! Tons of cash comes sliding back across the table. The man takes his winnings and buys the best room in the hotel. He sits the frog down and says, "Frog, I don't know how to repay you. You've won me all this money and I am forever grateful." The frog replies, "Ribbit Kiss Me." He figures why not, since after all, the frog did for him, he deserves it. With a kiss, the frog turns into a gorgeous 17-year-old girl. "And that, your honor, is how the girl ended up in my room. So help me God or my name is not William Jefferson Clinton."

The Clinton Anagram

"President Clinton of the USA" can be rearranged (with no letters left over, and using each letter only once) into:
"To copulate he finds interns"

A History Lesson About Lincoln And Kennedy

Make sure you read the whole thing because there is a twist at the end -
Think about this.......
Abraham Lincoln was elected to Congress in 1846.
John F. Kennedy was elected to Congress in 1946.
Abraham Lincoln was elected President in 1860.
John F. Kennedy was elected President in 1960.
The names Lincoln and Kennedy each contain seven letters.
Both were particularly concerned with civil rights.
Both wives lost their children while living in the White House.
Both Presidents were shot on a Friday.
Both were shot in the head.
Lincoln's secretary was named Kennedy.
Kennedy's secretary was named Lincoln.
Both were assassinated by Southerners.
Both were succeeded by Southerners.
Both Successors were named Johnson.
Andrew Johnson, who succeeded Lincoln, was born in 1808.
Lyndon Johnson, who succeeded Kennedy was born in 1908.
John Wilkes Booth, who assassinated Lincoln was born in 1839.
Lee Harvey Oswald, who assassinated Kennedy was born in 1939.
Both assassins were known by their three names.
Both names comprise of fifteen letters.
Booth ran from the theater and was caught in a warehouse.
Oswald ran from a warehouse and was caught in a theater.
Both assassins were assassinated before their trials.

And, Last but not least.......
A week before Lincoln was shot he was in Monroe, Maryland.
A week before Kennedy was shot he was in Marilyn Monroe.

DNA Results

Federal Bureau of Investigation Washington, DC:

Dear Mr. Kenneth Starr:
The test on Miss Lewinsky's dress came back inconclusive. Everyone in Arkansas
has the same DNA.
Sorry,
FBI

Simplified 1040

LATEST REVISION FOR: 1040 FEDERAL INCOME TAX FORM 1998
RETURN DEPARTMENT OF THE INTERNAL REVENUE SERVICE

PART 1: INCOME

Your Social Security Number ___ -__- ____

1. How much money did you make last year? $ _ _ _ _ _ _._ _

2. Send it in.

3. If you have any questions or comments, please write them in the box provided.
[____]

Paying In For Taxes

There was a man who computed his taxes for 1998 and discovered that he owed $3407. He packaged up his payment and included this letter:

Dear IRS:
Enclosed is my 1998 Tax Return and payment. Please take note of the attached article from the USA Today newspaper. In the article, you will see that the Pentagon is paying $171.50 for hammers and NASA has paid $600.00 for a toilet seat. Please find enclosed four toilet seats (value $2400) and six hammers (value $1029). This brings my total payment to $3429.00. Please note the overpayment of $22.00 and apply it to the "Presidential Election Fund," as noted on my return. Might I suggest you the send the above mentioned fund a "1.5 inch screw." (See attached article...HUD paid $22.00 for a 1.5 inch Phillips Head Screw.) It has been a pleasure to pay my tax bill this year, and I look forward to paying it again next year.

Sincerely,
A satisfied taxpayer

Relationships

Dave Goes To The Strip Club

Dave works hard at the plant and spends most evenings bowling or playing basketball at the gym. His wife thinks he is pushing himself too hard, so for his birthday she takes him to a local strip club. The doorman at the club greets them and says, "Hey, Dave, how ya doin?" His wife is puzzled and asks if he's been to this club before. "Oh no," says Dave. "He's on my bowling team." When they are seated, a waitress asks Dave if he'd like his usual Budweiser. His wife is becoming uncomfortable and says, "You must come here a lot for that woman to know you drink Budweiser." "No, honey, she's in the Ladies Bowling League. We share lanes with them." A stripper comes over to their table and throws her arms around Dave. "Hi Davey," she says, "want your usual table dance?" Dave's wife, now furious, grabs her purse and storms out of the club. Dave follows and spots her getting into a cab. Before she can slam the door, he jumps in beside her and she starts screaming at him. The cabby turns his head and says, "Looks like you picked up a real bitch tonight, Dave."

A Boy And His Date

A boy and his date were parked on a back road some distance from town, doing what boys and girls do on back roads some distance from town. Things were getting hot and heavy when the girl stopped the boy. "I really should have mentioned this earlier, but I'm actually a hooker and I charge $20 for sex," she said. The boy just looked at her for a couple of seconds, but then reluctantly paid her, and they did their thing. After the cigarette, the boy just sat in the driver's seat looking out the window. "Why aren't we going anywhere?" asked the girl. "Well, I should have mentioned this before, but I'm actually a taxi driver, and the fare back to town is $25."

Sean's Dyin' Wish

Sean was lyin' on his deathbed with his lifelong friend by his side. "Paddy, me dear friend, ye remember that grand case o' scotch we won at poker when we were in the merchant marine these many years ago?" "Aye, Sean, that I do. Some thirty years ago it was." "Well, laddie, I never told ye, but I set one bottle aside, and I've kept it even to this day." "Ah, Sean, heart of me heart, 'tis a fine thing ye've done!" Paddy's mouth was watering at the thought of having a last drink with his bosom buddy, a shot of magnificently aged whiskey. With great difficulty, Sean raised himself up on one elbow, reached out and clutched Paddy by the lapel of his jacket and looked him straight in the eye. "Paddy, me own, would ye do me one last, dyin' favor, in the name of our true and lastin' friendship?" Paddy returned his gaze with genuine affection. "Anything, Sean, ye know ye can count on me." Sean relaxed and fell back into his bed. "When they lay me out in that pine box and they lower me down into the ground and they cover me over with sod, Paddy, me boy, will ye take that fine bottle of scotch and pull the cork, and pour the whiskey all over me grave?" (pause as Paddy swallows)
"Aye, Sean, that I will ... But, would ye mind if it passes through me kidneys first?"

<u>The Perfect Couple</u>

Once upon a time, a perfect man and a perfect woman met. After a perfect courtship, they had a perfect wedding. Their life together was, of course, perfect. One snowy, stormy Christmas Eve, this perfect couple was driving their perfect car (a Subaru Legacy) along a winding road, when they noticed someone at the side of the road in distress. Being the perfect couple they stopped to help. There stood Santa Claus with a huge bundle of toys. Not wanting to disappoint any children on the eve of Christmas, the perfect couple loaded Santa and his toys into their vehicle. Soon, they were driving along delivering the toys. Unfortunately, the driving conditions deteriorated and the perfect couple and Santa Claus had an accident. Only one of them survived the accident. Who was the survivor?

(Scroll down for the answer.)

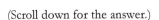

The perfect woman. She's the only one who really existed in the first place. Everyone knows there is no Santa Claus and there is no such a thing as a perfect man.

Women, end e-mail here. Men, keep scrolling.

So, if there is no perfect man and no Santa Claus, the perfect woman must have been driving. This explains why there was a car accident.

By the way, if you're a woman and you're reading this, this brings up another point: Women never listen either.

How To Impress A Woman:

Compliment her,

cuddle her,

kiss her,

caress her,

love her,

stroke her,

tease her,

comfort her,

protect her,

hug her,

hold her,

spend money on her,

wine and dine her,

buy things for her,

listen to her,

care for her,

stand by her,

support her,

go to the ends of the earth for her....

How To Impress A Man:

Show up naked.

The Silver Gravy Ladle

John invited his mother over for dinner. During the meal, his mother couldn't help noticing how attractive and shapely the housekeeper was. Over the course of the evening, she started to wonder if there was more between John and the housekeeper than met the eye. Reading his mom's thoughts, John volunteered, "I know what you must be thinking, but I assure you, my relationship with my housekeeper is purely professional." About a week later, the housekeeper came to John and said, "Ever since your mother came to dinner, I've been unable to find the beautiful silver gravy ladle. You don't suppose she took it, do you?" John said, "Well, I doubt it, but I'll write her a letter just to be sure." So he sat down and wrote:

"Dear Mother,
    I'm not saying you 'did' take a gravy ladle from my house, and I'm not saying you 'did not' take a gravy ladle. But, the fact remains that one has been missing ever since you were here for dinner.
Love, John"

Several days later, John received a letter from his mother which said:

"Dear Son,
    I'm not saying that you 'do' sleep with your housekeeper, and I'm not saying that you 'do not' sleep with your housekeeper. But, the fact remains that if she was sleeping in her own bed, she would have found the gravy ladle by now.
Love, Mom"

A man and a woman are in a car accident...

...Both of their cars are totally demolished, but amazingly neither of them is hurt. After they crawl out of their cars, the woman says, "Wow, just look at our cars! There's nothing left, but fortunately we are unhurt. And, you're a man and I'm a woman. This must be a sign from God that we should meet and be friends and live together in peace for the rest of our days." Flattered, the man replied, "Oh yes, I agree with you completely!" "This must be a sign from God!" The woman continued, "And, look at this, here's another miracle. My car is completely demolished but this bottle of wine didn't break. Surely God wants us to drink this wine and celebrate our good fortune." Then, she hands the bottle to the man. The man nods his head in agreement, opens it and drinks half the bottle and then hands it back to the woman. The woman takes the bottle, immediately puts the cap back on, and hands it back to the man. The man asks, "Aren't you having any?" The woman replies, "No. I think I'll just wait for the police."

The Motorcycle Repair

A man was working on his motorcycle on his patio and his wife was in the house in the kitchen. The man was racing the engine on the motorcycle and somehow, the motorcycle slipped into gear. The man, still holding the handlebars, was dragged through a glass patio door and the motorcycle dumped onto the floor inside the house. The wife, hearing the crash, ran into the dining room, and found her husband lying on the floor, cut and bleeding, the motorcycle lying next to him and the patio door shattered. The wife ran to the phone and summoned an ambulance. Because they lived on a fairly large hill, the wife went down the several flights of long steps to the street to direct the paramedics to her husband. After the ambulance arrived and transported the husband to the hospital, the wife uprighted the motorcycle and pushed it outside. Seeing that gas had spilled on the floor, the wife obtained some papers towels, blotted up the gasoline, and threw the towels in the toilet.

The husband was treated at the hospital and was released to come home. After arriving home, he looked at the shattered patio door and the damage done to his motorcycle. He became despondent, went into the bathroom, sat on the toilet and smoked a cigarette. After finishing the cigarette, he flipped it between his legs into the toilet bowl while still seated. The wife, who was in the kitchen, heard a loud explosion and her husband screaming. She ran into the bathroom and found her husband lying on the floor. His trousers had been blown away and he was suffering burns on the buttocks, the back of his legs and his groin. The wife again ran to the phone and called for an ambulance. The same ambulance crew was dispatched and the wife met them at the street. The paramedics loaded the husband on the stretcher and began carrying him to the street. While they were going down the stairs to the street accompanied by the wife, one of the paramedics asked the wife how the husband had burned himself. She told them and the paramedics started laughing so hard, one of them tipped the stretcher and dumped the husband out. He fell down the remaining steps and broke his ankle.

Two Italian Men On The Bus

A bus stops and two Italian men get on. They seat themselves and engage in animated conversation. The lady sitting behind them ignores their conversation at first, but her attention is galvanized when she hears one of the men say, "Emma come first. Den I come. Two asses, they come together. I come again. Two asses, they come together again. I come again and pee twice. Then, I come once-a-more." "You foul-mouthed swine," retorted the lady indignantly. "In this country we don't talk about our sex lives in public!" Hey, coola down lady," said the man, "Imma justa tellun my friend howa to spella Mississippi."

Getting A Haircut

Women's version:

Woman1: Oh! You got a haircut! That's so cute!

Woman2: Do you think so? I wasn't sure when she gave me the mirror. I mean, you don't think it's too fluffy looking?

Woman1: Oh God no! No, it's perfect. I'd love to get my hair cut like that, but I think my face is too wide. I'm pretty much stuck with this stuff I think.

Woman2: Are you serious? I think your face is adorable. And, you could easily get one of those layer cuts that would look so cute I think. I was actually going to do that except that I was afraid it would accent my long neck.

Woman1: Oh - that's funny! I would love to have your neck! Anything to take attention away from this two-by-four I have for a shoulder line.

Woman2: Are you kidding? I know girls that would love to have your shoulders. Everything drapes so well on you. I mean, look at my arms see how short they are? If I had your shoulders I could get clothes to fit me so much easier.

Men's version:

Man1: Haircut?

Man2: Yeah.

Stand By Your Man

The woman's husband had been slipping in and out of a coma for several months, yet she had stayed by his bedside every single day. One day, when he came to, he motioned for her to come nearer. As she sat by him, he whispered, eyes full of tears, "My dearest, you have been with me all through the bad times. When I got fired, you were there to support me. When my business failed, you were there. When I got shot, you were by my side. When we lost the house, you stayed right here. When my health started failing, you were still by my side. You know what?" "What dear?" she gently asked, smiling as her heart began to fill with warmth. "I think you're bad luck."

Her Story, His Story

A girl and boy in a relationship of about four months now. One Friday night, they meet at a bar after work. They stay for a few drinks, then go to get some food at a local restaurant near their respective homes. They eat, then go back to his house and she stays over.

Her story: He was in an odd mood when I got to the bar. I thought it might have been because I was a bit late but he didn't say anything much about it. The conversation was quite slow going so I thought we should go off somewhere more intimate so we could talk more privately. So, we went to this restaurant and he's STILL a bit funny and I'm trying to cheer him up and start to wonder whether it's me or something else. I ask him, and he says no. But, you know I'm not really sure. So anyway, in the cab back to his house, I say that I love him and he just puts his arm around me. I don't know what the hell this means because you know he doesn't say it back or anything. We finally get back to his place I'm wondering if he's getting tired of me! So, I try to ask him about it but he just switches on the TV. So, I say I'm going to go to sleep. Then, after about 10 minutes, he joins me and we have sex. But, he still seems really distracted, so afterwards I just want to leave. I dunno. I just don't know what he thinks anymore. I mean, do you think he's met someone else???

His story: Crappy day at work, low on funds, and tired. Got laid though.

Religion

A Fish Tale

A priest decides to take a walk to the pier near his church. He looks around and finally stops to watch a fisherman load his boat. The fisherman notices, and asks the priest if he would like to join him for a couple of hours. The priest agrees. The fisherman asks if the priest has ever fished before, to which the priest says no. He baits the hook for him and says, "Give it a shot father." After a few minutes, the priest hooks a big fish and struggles to get it in the boat.

The *fisherman* says "Whoa, what a big sonofabitch!"
Priest: "Uh, please sir, can you mind your language?"
Fisherman: (THINKING QUICKLY) "I'm sorry father, but that's what this fish is
    called - a sonofabitch!"
Priest: "Oh, I'm sorry - I didn't know."

After the trip, the priest brings the fish to the church and spots the bishop.
Priest: "Eminence, look at this big sonofabitch!"
Bishop: "Please Father, mind your language, this is a house of God."
Priest: "No, you don't understand - that's what this fish is called, and I caught it. I
    caught this sonofabitch!"
Bishop: "Hmmm. You know. I could clean this sonofabitch and we could have it
for dinner."

So, the Bishop takes the fish and cleans it, and brings it to Mother Superior at the convent.
Bishop: "Mother Superior could you cook this sonofabitch for dinner tonight?"
Mother Superior: "My lord, what language!"
Bishop: "No, Sister, that's what the fish is called - a sonofabitch! Father caught it, I
    cleaned it, and we'd like you to cook it."

Well, the Pope stops by for dinner with the three of them, and they all think the fish is great. He asks where they got it.
Priest: "I caught the sonofabitch!"
Bishop: "And, I cleaned the sonofabitch!"
Mother Superior: "And, I cooked the sonofabitch!"
The **Pope** stares at them for a minute with a steely gaze, but then takes off his hat, puts his feet up on the table, and says, "You know, you f***ers are all right."

Serenity Prayer

"Grant me the serenity to accept things I cannot change; the courage to change things I cannot accept; the wisdom to hide the bodies of those people that I had to kill today because they ticked me off; and also help me to be careful of the toes I step on today as they may be connected to the butt that I may have to kiss tomorrow."

Noah And Today's Ark

The Lord spoke to Noah and said, "Noah, in six months I am going to make it rain until the whole world is covered with water and all the evil things are destroyed. But, I want to save a few good people and two of every living thing on the planet. I am ordering you to build an ark." And, in a flash of lightning, he delivered the specifications for the ark. "OK," Noah said, trembling with fear and fumbling with the blueprints, "I'm your man." "Six months and it starts to rain," thundered the Lord. "You better have my ark completed or learn to swim for a long, long time!" Six months passed, the sky began to cloud up, and the rain began to fall in torrents. The Lord looked down and saw Noah sitting in his yard, weeping, and there was no ark.

"Noah!" shouted the Lord, "Where is My ark?" A lightning bolt crashed into the ground right beside Noah. "Lord, please forgive me!" begged Noah. "I did my best, but there were some big problems. First, I had to get a building permit for the ark's construction, but your plans did not meet their code. So, I had to hire an engineer to redo the plans, only to get into a long argument with him about whether to include a fire-sprinkler system." "My neighbors objected, claiming that I was violating zoning ordinances by building the ark in my front yard, so I had to get a variance from the city planning board." "Then, I had a big problem getting enough wood for the ark, because there was a ban on cutting trees to save the spotted owl. I tried to convince the environmentalists and the U.S. Fish and Wildlife Service that I needed the wood to save the owls, but they wouldn't let me catch them, so no owls."

"Next, I started gathering up the animals but got sued by an animal rights group that objected to me taking along only two of each kind." "Just when the suit got dismissed, the EPA notified me that I couldn't complete the ark without filing an environmental impact statement on your proposed flood. They didn't take kindly to the idea that they had no jurisdiction over the conduct of a Supreme Being." "Then, the Corps of Engineers wanted a map of the proposed flood plan. I sent them a globe!" "Right now, I'm still trying to resolve a complaint with the Equal Opportunities Commission over how many minorities I'm supposed to hire." "The IRS has seized all my assets claiming that I am trying to leave the country, and I just got a notice from the state that I owe some kind of use tax. Really, I don't think I can finish the ark in less than five years." With that, the sky cleared, the sun began to shine, and a rainbow arched across the sky. Noah looked up and smiled. "You mean you are not going to destroy the world?" he asked hopefully. "No," said the Lord, "the government already has."

Magic Elevator

An Amish boy and his father were visiting a mall. They were amazed before almost everything they saw, but especially by two shiny, silver walls that could move apart and back together again. The boy asked his father, "What is this father?" The father (never having seen an elevator) responded, "Son, I have never seen anything like this in my life. I don't know what it is." While the boy and his father were watching wide-eyed, an old lady in a wheelchair rolled up to the moving walls and pressed a button. The walls opened and the lady rolled between them and into a small room. The walls closed and the boy and his father watched small circles of light with numbers above the wall light up. They continued to watch the circles light up in the reverse direction. The walls opened up again and a beautiful young woman stepped out. The father said to his son, "Go get your Mother."

Anything Can Be Found In The Bible

During his sermon on Sunday, the local preacher told his congregation that the entire range of human existence could be found in the Bible. "If anything can happen to humans, it is described in the Bible." After the service, a woman came up to the preacher and said, "Reverend, I don't think the Bible mentions anything about PMS anywhere." The preacher told the woman he was certain he could find reference to PMS somewhere in the Bible. During the following week, he searched diligently, book-by-book, chapter-by-chapter, and verse-by-verse. On the following Sunday, the woman came up to him and asked, "Did you find PMS mentioned in the Bible?" The preacher smiled, opened his Bible, and began to read, "...and Mary rode Joseph's ass all the way to Bethlehem."

Ford vs. Adam

Henry Ford dies and goes to heaven. At the pearly gates, the angel tells Ford, "Well, you've been such a good guy and your invention, the car, revolutionized the world. As a reward, you can hang out with anyone you want in heaven." So, Henry Ford thinks about it and says, "I wanna hang with Adam, the first man." So, the guy at the gates points Adam out to Ford. When Ford gets to Adam, Ford asks, "Hey, aren't you the inventor of the woman?" Adam says yes. "Well," says Ford, "you have some major design flaws in your invention:
1. There's too much front end protrusion.
2. It chatters at high speeds.
3. The rear end wobbles too much.
4. And, the intake is placed too close to the exhaust."

"Hmmm...," says Adam, "hold on." So, Adam goes to the celestial super computer, types in a few keystrokes, and waits for the result. The computer prints out a clip of paper and Adam reads it. He then says to Henry Ford, "It may be that my invention is flawed, but according to the stellar computer, more men are riding my invention than yours."

Honk If You Love Jesus

The other day, I went to the local religious book store, where I saw a "HONK IF YOU LOVE JESUS" bumper sticker. I bought it and put it on the back bumper of my car, and I'm really glad I did. What an uplifting experience followed. I was stopped at the light at a busy intersection, just lost in thought about the Lord, and didn't notice that the light had changed. That bumper sticker really worked! I found lots of people who love Jesus. Why, the guy behind me started to honk like crazy. He must REALLY love the lord because pretty soon, he leaned out his window and yelled, "Jesus Christ!!" as loud as he could. It was like a football game with him shouting, "GO JESUS CHRIST, GO!!!" Everyone else started honking, too, so I leaned out my window and waved and smiled to all of those loving people. There must have been a guy from Florida back there because I could hear him yelling something about a sunny beach, and saw him waving in a funny way with only his middle finger stuck up in the air. I asked my two kids what that meant. They kind of squirmed, looked at each other, giggled and told me that it was the Hawaiian good luck sign. So, I leaned out the window and gave him the good luck sign back.

Several cars behind, a very nice young man stepped out of his car and yelled something. I couldn't hear him very well, but it sounded like, "Mother trucker," or "Mother's from there." Maybe he was from Florida, too. He must really love the lord. A couple of the people were so caught up in the joy of the moment that they got out of their cars and were walking toward me. I bet they wanted to pray, but just then I noticed that the light had changed, and stepped on the gas. And, a good thing I did, because I was the only driver to get across the intersection. I looked back at them standing there. I leaned way out the window, gave them a big smile and held up the Hawaiian good luck sign, as I drove away. Praise the Lord for such wonderful folks.

The Spiritualist Lovers

There were two lovers, who were really into spiritualism and reincarnation. They vowed that if either died, the other one remaining would try to contact the partner in the other world exactly 30 days after their death. Unfortunately, a few weeks later, the young man died in a car wreck. True to her word, his sweetheart tried to contact him in the spirit world exactly 30 days later. At the seance, she called out, "John, John, this is Martha. Do you hear me?" A ghostly voice answered her, "Yes Martha, this is John. I can hear you." Martha tearfully asked, "Oh John, what is it like where you are?" "It's beautiful. There are azure skies, a soft breeze, sunshine most of the time." "What do you do all day?" asked Martha. "Well, Martha, we get up before sunrise, eat some good breakfast, and there's nothing but making love until noon. After lunch, we nap until two and then make love again until about five. After dinner, we go at it again until we fall asleep about 11 p.m." Martha was somewhat taken aback. "Is that what heaven really is like?" "Heaven? I'm not in heaven, Martha." "Well, then, where are you?" "I'm a rabbit in Arizona."

The 7 Dwarfs Meet The Pope

Six of the seven dwarfs are sitting around the house one day when Sleepy rushes in and says, "Guess what guys, I've won a trip to see the Pope!" Everyone gets all excited and chants, "We finally get to ask him, we finally get to ask him." The next day, they are standing in front of the Pope, Dopey out in front of the other six. All the other six start pushing Dopey and saying, "Go ahead, Dopey, ask him, ask him!" The Pope looks at Dopey and asks, "Do you have a question to ask me, young man?" Dopey looks up shyly and says, "Well, yes." The Pope tells him to go ahead and ask. Dopey asks, "Well, do....do they have nuns in Alaska?" The Pope replies, "Well, yes, I'm sure we have nuns in Alaska." The others all keep nudging Dopey and chanting, "Ask him the rest, Dopey, ask him the rest!" The Pope asks Dopey if there's more to his question, and Dopey continues, "Well, uh, do they have, uh, black nuns in Alaska?" To which the Pope replies, "Well, my son, I think there must be a few black nuns in Alaska, yes." Still not satisfied, the others keep saying, "Ask him the last part, Dopey, ask him the last part!" The Pope asks Dopey, "Is there still more to your question?" To which Dopey replies, "Well, uh, yeah..... are there, uh, are there any midget black nuns in Alaska?" The startled Pope replies, "Well, no, my son, I really don't think there are any midget black nuns in Alaska." At this, Dopey turns all kinds of colors, and the others start laughing and yelling, "Dopey screwed a penguin, Dopey screwed a penguin!"

The New Parishioners

Three couples; an elderly couple, a middle-aged couple and a young newlywed couple wanted to join a church. The pastor said, "We have special requirements for new parishioners. You must abstain from having sex for two weeks." The couples agreed and came back at the end of two weeks. The pastor went to the elderly couple and asked, "Were you able to abstain from sex for the two weeks?" The old man replied, "No problem at all, Pastor." "Congratulations! Welcome to the church!" said the pastor. The pastor went to the middle-aged couple and asked, "Well, were you able to abstain from sex for the two weeks?" The man replied, "The first week was not too bad. The second week I had to sleep on the couch for a couple of nights but, yes we made it." "Congratulations! Welcome to the church!" said the pastor. The pastor then went to the newlywed couple and asked, "Well, were you able to abstain from sex for two weeks?" "No Pastor, we were not able to go without sex for the two weeks," the young man replied sadly. "What happened?" inquired the pastor. "My wife was reaching for a can of corn on the top shelf and dropped it. When she bent over to pick it up, I was overcome with lust and took advantage of her right there." "You understand, of course, this means you will not be welcome in our church," stated the pastor. "We know," said the young man. "We're not welcome at the grocery store anymore either."

Catholic Math

Little Tommy was doing very badly in math. His parents had tried everything; tutors, flash cards, special learning centers, in short, everything they could think of. Finally, in a last ditch effort, they took Tommy down and enrolled him in the local Catholic School. After the first day, little Tommy comes home with a very serious look on his face. He doesn't kiss his mother hello. Instead, he goes straight to his room and starts studying. Books and papers are spread out all over the room and little Tommy is hard at work. His mother is amazed. She calls him down to dinner and to her shock, the minute he is done he marches back to his room without a word and in no time he is back hitting the books as hard as before. This goes on for sometime, day after day while the mother tries to understand what made all the difference. Finally, little Tommy brings home his report card. He quietly lays it on the table and goes up to his room and hits the books. With great trepidation, his mom looks at it and to her surprise, little Tommy got an A in math. She can no longer hold her curiosity. She goes to his room and says, "Son, what was it? Was it the nuns?" Little Tommy looks at her and shakes his head. "Well then," she replies, "was it the books, the discipline, the structure, the uniforms, WHAT was it?" Little Tommy looks at her and says, "Well, on the first day of school, when I saw that guy nailed to the plus sign, I knew they weren't fooling around."

An Engineer Dies

An engineer dies and reports to the pearly gates. St. Peter checks his dossier and says, "Ah, I can't find your name, you're in the wrong place." So the engineer reports to the gates of hell and is let in. Pretty soon, the engineer gets dissatisfied with the level of comfort in hell, and starts designing and building improvements. After a while, they've got air conditioning and flush toilets and escalators, and the engineer is a pretty popular guy. One day, God calls Satan up on the telephone and says with a sneer, "So, how's it going down there in hell?" Satan replies, "Hey, things are going great. We've got air conditioning and flush toilets and escalators, and there's no telling what this engineer is going to come up with next." God replies, "What??? You've got an engineer? That's a mistake…he should never have gotten down there; send him up here." Satan says, "No way. I like having an engineer on the staff, and I'm keeping him." God says, "Send him back up here or I'll sue." Satan laughs uproariously and answers, "Yeah, right. And, just where are YOU going to get a lawyer?"

A Missionary And A Lion

A missionary was walking in Africa when he heard the ominous padding of a lion behind him. "Oh Lord," prayed the missionary, "grant in Thy goodness that the lion walking behind me is a good Christian lion." And then, in the silence that followed, the missionary heard the lion praying too, "Oh Lord," he prayed, "we thank thee for the food which we are about to receive."

Pick 3 Hymns

One Sunday, a pastor told his congregation that the church needed some extra money and asked the people to prayerfully consider giving a little extra in the offering plate. He said that whoever gave the most would be able to pick out three hymns. After the offering plates were passed, the pastor glanced down and noticed that someone had placed a $1,000 bill in offering. He was so excited that he immediately shared his joy with his congregation and said he'd like to personally thank the person who placed the money in the plate. A very quiet, elderly, saintly lady all the way in the back shyly raised her hand. The pastor asked her to come to the front. Slowly she made her way to the pastor. He told her how wonderful it was that she gave so much and in thanksgiving asked her to pick out three hymns. Her eyes brightened as she looked over the congregation, pointed to the three handsomest men in the building and said, "I'll take him and him and him."

Satan Visits A Church

One bright, beautiful Sunday morning, everyone in the tiny town of Johnstown got up early and went to the local church. Before the services started, the townspeople were sitting in their pews and talking about their lives, their families, etc. Suddenly, Satan appeared at the front of the church. Everyone started screaming and running for the front entrance, trampling each other in a frantic effort to get away from evil incarnate. Soon, everyone was evacuated from the Church, except for one elderly gentleman who sat calmly in his pew, not moving.....seemingly oblivious to the fact that God's ultimate enemy was in his presence. Now, this confused Satan a bit, so he walked up to the man and said, "Don't you know who I am?" The man replied, "Yep, sure do." Satan asked, "Aren't you afraid of me?" "Nope, sure ain't," said the man. Satan was a little perturbed at this and queried, "Why aren't you afraid of me?" The man calmly replied, "Been married to your sister for over 48 years."

Four Old College Friends

Four old college friends were having coffee. The first, a Catholic woman tells her friends, "My son is now a Priest. When he walks into a room, everyone calls him 'Father'." The second Catholic woman chirps, "My son is a Bishop. Whenever he walks into a room, people call him 'Your Grace'." The third Catholic crone says, "My son is a Cardinal. Whenever he walks into a room, he's called 'Your Eminence'." Since the fourth woman, a Jewish lady, sipped her coffee in silence, the first three women give her this subtle "Well...?" So she replies, "My son is 6' 6.". he has plenty of money...broad square shoulders ...terribly handsome...dresses very well...tight muscular body...tight hard buns... and whenever he walks into a room... women gasp, 'Oh, my God...'."

A Priest At His First Mass

A new priest at his first mass was so nervous he could hardly speak. After mass, he asked the monsignor how he had done. The monsignor replied, "When I am worried about getting nervous on the pulpit, I put a glass of vodka next to the water glass. If I start to get nervous, I take a sip." So, the next Sunday, he took the monsignor's advice. At the beginning of the sermon, he got nervous and took a drink. He proceeded to talk up a storm. Upon return to his office after mass, he found the following note on his door:

1. Sip the Vodka, don't gulp.
2. There are 10 commandments, not 12.
3. There are 12 disciples, not 10.
4. Jesus was consecrated, not constipated.
5. Jacob wagered his donkey, he did not bet his ass.
6. We do not refer to Jesus Christ as the late J.C.
7. The Father, Son, and Holy Ghost are not referred to as Daddy, Junior, and Spook.
8. David slew Goliath, he did not kick the crap out of him.
9. David was hit by a rock and knocked off his donkey; don't say he was stoned off his ass.
10. We do not refer to the cross as the Big T!
11. When Jesus broke the bread at the Last Supper he said, "Take this and eat it, for it is my body," he did not say, "Eat me."
12. The Virgin Mary is not referred to as the, "Mary with the Cherry."
13. The recommended grace before a meal is not: "Rub-A-dub-dub, thanks for the grub, yeah God!"
14. Next Sunday, there will be a taffy-pulling contest at St. Peter's, not a peter-pulling contest at St. Taffy's.

The Confessional

A drunk staggers into a church and sits down in a confessional and says nothing. The bewildered priest coughs to attract his attention, but still the man says nothing. The priest knocks on the wall three times in a final attempt to get the man to speak. The drunk replies, "No use knockin' mate, there's no paper in this one either."

Work or Play?

A man wonders if having sex on the Sabbath is a sin because he is not sure if sex is work or play. So, he goes to a priest and asks for his opinion on this question. After consulting the Bible, the priest says, "My son, after an exhaustive search, I am positive that sex is work and is therefore not permitted on Sundays." The man thinks, "What does a priest know about sex?" So, he goes to a minister, who after all is a married man and experienced in this matter. He queries the minister and receives the same reply. Sex is work and, therefore, not for the Sabbath! Not pleased with the reply, he seeks out a Rabbi, a man of thousands of years tradition and knowledge. The Rabbi ponders the question, then states, "My son, sex is definitely play." The man replies, "Rabbi, how can you be so sure when so many others tell me sex is work?" The Rabbi softly speaks, "My son, if sex were work, my wife would have the maid do it."

Too Little, Too Late

A New York divorce lawyer died and arrived at the pearly gates. Saint Peter asks him "What have you done to merit entrance into Heaven?" The lawyer thought a moment, then said, "A week ago, I gave a quarter to a homeless person on the street." Saint Peter asked Gabriel to check this out in the record, and after a moment Gabriel affirmed that this was true. Saint Peter said, "Well, that's fine, but it's not really quite enough to get you into Heaven." The lawyer said, "Wait! Wait! There's more! Three years ago I also gave a homeless person a quarter." Saint Peter nodded to Gabriel, who after a moment nodded back, affirming this, too, had been verified. Saint Peter then whispered to Gabriel, "Well, what do you suggest we do with this fellow?" Gabriel gave the lawyer a sidelong glance, then said to Saint Peter, "Let's give him back his 50 cents and tell him to go to Hell."

Sports

Pearly Gates

After Aaron Rodgers dies and enters the Pearly Gates, God takes him on a tour. He shows Aaron a little two-bedroom house with a faded Packer banner hanging from the front porch. "This is your house, Aaron. Most people don't get their own houses up here," God says. Aaron looks at the little house, then turns around and looks at another house sitting on top of the hill. It's a huge two-story mansion with white marble columns and a patio under all the windows, Minnesota flags line both sides of the sidewalk and a huge Vikings banner hangs between the marble columns. "Thanks for the house, God, but let me ask you a question. I get this little two-bedroom house with faded banners and Randall Cunningham gets a mansion with brand new Vikings banners and flags flying all over the place. Why is that?" God looks at him seriously for a moment, then with a smile, says, "That's not Cunningham's house, it's mine!"

The Iron Grip

It was Olympics time and the Russians had sent their best man to compete in the wrestling competition. This man was famous for one thing, and that was the "Iron Grip." If he got anyone into that grip, then they were dead-meat. The Swedes were studying videos of this wrestler and they realized that if their competitor managed to avoid falling into this "Iron Grip," they could win. The best of the Swedes finally made it to the finals, and so did the Russian. It started well, the Swede managing to get in a couple of points. Then, when there was only a half minute left, the Russian managed to get the Swede into his "Iron Grip." The Swedish coach walked, totally depressed, back to the locker room. All of a sudden, he heard the crowd roar outside, "Sverige! Sverige! Sverige!"

The wrestler entered the locker room cheering. The coach looked at him in shock and asked, "How did you get out of the 'Iron Grip'?" The wrestler was gasping air and said, "Well, as I was lying there, trying to get out of it, I saw these two nuts just hanging there in front of me, and I just thought, 'This is the Olympics. It is only held every 4th year. This is my big chance. It's now or never.' So, I grabbed 'em with my free hand and squeezed as hard as I could. And, I promise you one thing, if you squeeze your own balls that hard you can get out of any grip."

Golf vs. Skydiving

What's the difference between a bad golfer and a bad skydiver?

Bad Golfer: "Whack!" "Shit!"

Bad Skydiver: "Shit!!" "Whack!!"

A Golfing Physical Therapist

A couple of women were playing golf one sunny Saturday morning. The first of the twosome teed-off and watched in horror as the ball headed directly toward a foursome of men playing the next hole. Indeed, the ball hit one of the men and he immediately clasped his hands together at his crotch, fell to the ground and proceeded to roll around in agony. The woman rushed down to the man and immediately began to apologize. She then explained that she was a physical therapist and offered to help ease his "pain." "Please allow me to help. I'm a physical therapist and I know I could relieve your pain if you'd just allow me!," she told him earnestly. "Ummph, oooh, nnooo, I'll be alright...I'll be fine in a few minutes," he replied as he remained in the fetal position still clasping his hands together at his crotch. The woman takes it upon herself to begin to "ease his pain." She began to massage his groin. After a few moments she asked, "Does that feel better?" The man looked up at her and replied, "Yes, that feels pretty good...but my thumb still hurts like hell!"

Football Fans On The Train

There's a Vikings fan, a Packers fan, and a beautiful woman sitting next to each other on a train. The train goes through a tunnel and everything gets dark. Suddenly, there is a kissing sound and then a slap! The train comes out of the tunnel. The woman and the Vikings fan are sitting there looking perplexed. The Packers fan is bent over, holding his face which is red from an apparent slap. The Packers fan is thinking, "Wow, that Vikings fan must have tried to kiss this lady. She thought it was me and slapped me." The lady is thinking, "That Packer fan must have moved to kiss me but kissed the Vikings fan instead and got slapped." The Vikings fan was thinking to himself..."If this train goes through another tunnel, I'm gonna make another kissing sound and slap that Packers fan again."

Golf And Mother Nature

Two guys are out one day golfing. One slices off to the right, one hooks off to the left and they both go to retrieve their balls. The guy on the right is hacking and hacking at the ball but just can't lift it out of the buttercups. It has become lodged in. All of a sudden, up from the ground comes Mother Nature and is she mad! "What the hell are you doing to my beautiful buttercups?" she asks. "I'm just trying to get my golf ball out of them, lady," replies the golfer. "Well, you are really making me mad. Just look what you've done to my buttercups. For this I must punish you. Your punishment will be an entire year without butter!" The golfer starts laughing hysterically which by now has just about worn out Mother Nature's patience. "What in the hell do you think is so funny about no butter for a year?" she screams at him. "I'm not laughing about that. I'm laughing about my friend over there whacking the hell out of your pussy willows!"

Technology

Tech Support Issues

Customer: "I got this problem. You people sent me this install disk, and now my A: drive won't work."

Tech Support: "Your A: drive won't work?"

Customer: "That's what I said. You sent me a bad disk, it got stuck in my drive, now it won't work at all."

Tech Support: "Did it not install properly? What kind of error messages did you get?"

Customer: "I didn't get any error message. The disk got stuck in the drive and wouldn't come out. So I got these pliers and tried to get it out. That didn't work either."

Tech Support: "You did what sir?"

Customer: "I got these pliers, and tried to get the disk out, but it wouldn't budge. I just ended up cracking the plastic stuff a bit."

Tech Support: "I don't understand sir, did you push the eject button?"

Customer: "No, so then I got a stick of butter and melted it and used a turkey baster and put the butter in the drive, around the disk, and that got it loose. I can't believe you would send me a disk that was broke and defective."

Tech Support: "Let me get this clear. You put melted butter in your A: drive and used pliers to pull the disk out?"

(At this point, I put the call on the speaker phone and motioned at the other techs to listen in.)

Tech Support: "Just so I am absolutely clear on this, can you repeat what you just said?"

Customer: "I said I put butter in my A: drive to get your crappy disk out, then I had to use pliers to pull it out."

Tech Support: "Did you push that little button that was sticking out when the disk was in the drive, you know, the thing called the disk eject button?"

Silence.

Tech Support: "Sir?"

Customer: "Yes."

Tech Support: "Sir, did you push the eject button?"

Customer: "No, but you people are going to fix my computer, or I am going to sue you for breaking my computer!"

Tech Support: "Let me get this straight. You are going to sue our company because you put the disk in the A: drive, didn't follow the instructions we sent you, didn't actually seek professional advice, didn't consult your user's manual on how to use your computer properly, instead proceeding to pour butter into the drive and physically rip the disk out?"

Customer: "Ummmm."

Tech Support: "Do you really think you stand a chance, since we record every call and have it on tape?"

Customer: (now rather humbled) "But you're supposed to help!"

Tech Support: "I am sorry sir, but there is nothing we can do for you. Have a nice day."

****

At 3:37 a.m. on a Sunday, I had just looked at the clock to determine my annoyance level, when I received a frantic phone call from a new user of a Macintosh Plus. She had gotten her entire family out of the house and was calling from her neighbor's. She had just received her first system error and interpreted the picture of the bomb on the screen as a warning that the computer was going to blow up.

****

Tech Support: "I need you to right-click on the Open Desktop."
Customer: "OK."
Tech Support: "Did you get a pop-up menu?"
Customer: "No."
Tech Support: "OK. Right click again. Do you see a pop-up menu?"
Customer: "No."
Tech Support: "OK, sir. Can you tell me what you have done up until this point?"
Customer: "Sure, you told me to write 'click' and I wrote click.'"
(At this point I had to put the caller on hold to tell the rest of the tech support staff what had happened. I couldn't, however, stop from giggling when I got back to the call.)
Tech Support: "OK, did you type 'click' with the keyboard?"
Customer: "I have done something dumb, right?"

****

One woman called Dell's toll-free line to ask how to install the batteries in her laptop. When told that the directions were on the first page of the manual the woman replied angrily, "I just paid $2,000 for this damn thing, and I'm not going to read the book."

****

Customer: "I received the software update you sent, but I am still getting the same error message."
Tech Support: "Did you install the update?"
Customer: "No. Oh, am I supposed to install it to get it to work?"

****

Customer: "Uhh.....I need help unpacking my new PC."
Tech Support: "What exactly is the problem?"
Customer: "I can't open the box."
Tech Support: "Well, I'd remove the tape holding the box closed and go from there."
Customer: "Uhhhh.....OK, thanks..."

Tech Support: "OK, in the bottom left hand side of the screen, can you see the 'OK' button displayed?"
Customer: "Wow ! How can you see my screen from there?"

****

Customer: "I'm having trouble installing Microsoft Word."
Tech Support: "Tell me what you've done."
Customer: "I typed 'A:SETUP'."
Tech Support: "Ma'am, remove the disk and tell me what it says."
Customer: "It says '[PC manufacturer] Restore and Recovery disk.'"
Tech Support: "Insert the MS Word setup disk."
Customer: "What?"
Tech Support: "Did you buy MS word?"
Customer: "No . . . ."

****

Customer: "I'm having a problem installing your software. I've got a fairly old computer, and when I type 'INSTALL,' all it says is 'Bad command or file name'."
Tech Support: "OK, check the directory of the A: drive. Go to A:\ and type 'dir'."
Customer reads off a list of file names, including 'INSTALL.EXE'.
Tech Support: "All right, the correct file is there. Type 'INSTALL' again."
Customer: "OK." (pause) "Still says, 'Bad command or file name'."
Tech Support: "Hmmm. The file's there in the correct place. It can't help but do something. Are you sure you're typing I-N-S-T-A-L-L and hitting the Enter key?"
Customer: "Yes, let me try it again." (pause) "Nope, still 'Bad command or file name'."
Tech Support: (now really confused) "Are you sure you're typing I-N-S-T-A-L-L and hitting the key that says 'Enter'?"
Customer: "Well, yeah. Although my 'N' key is stuck, so I'm using the 'M' key…..does that matter?

****

At our company we have asset numbers on the front of everything. They give the location, name, and everything else just by scanning the computer's asset barcode or using the number beneath the bars.
Customer: "Hello. I can't get on the network."
Tech Support: "OK. Just read me your asset number so we can open an outage."
Customer: "What is that?"
Tech Support: "That little barcode on the front of your computer."
Customer: "OK. Big bar, little bar, big bar, big bar….."

Tech Support Request

Tech Support,

Last year, I upgraded Girlfriend 1.0 to Wife 1.0 and noticed that the new program began unexpected child processing that took up a lot of space and valuable resources. No mention of this phenomenon was included in the product brochure. In addition, Wife 1.0 installs itself into all other programs and launches during system initialization where it monitors all other system activity. Applications such as Pokernight 10.3 and Beerbash 2.5 no longer run, crashing the system whenever selected. I can not seem to purge Wife 1.0 from my system. I am thinking about going back to Girlfriend 1.0 but un-install does not work on this program. Can you help me?

-Jonathan Powell

Dear Jonathan Powell,

This is a very common problem men complain about but is mostly due to a primary misconception. Many people upgrade from Girlfriend 1.0 to Wife 1.0 with the idea that Wife 1.0 is merely a "UTILITIES & ENTERTAINMENT" program. Wife 1.0 is an OPERATING SYSTEM and designed by its creator to run everything. WARNING DO NOT TRY TO: un-install, delete, or purge the program from the system once installed. Trying to un-install Wife 1.0 can be disastrous. Doing so may destroy your hard and/or floppy drive. Trying to un-install or remove Wife 1.0 will destroy valuable system resources. You can not go back to Girlfriend 1.0 because Wife 1.0 is not designed to do this. Some have tried to install Girlfriend 2.0 or Wife 2.0 but end up with more problems than the original system. Look in your manual under Warnings- Alimony/Child Support. Others have tried to run Girlfriend 1.0 in the background, while Wife 1.0 is running. Eventually, Wife 1.0 detects Girlfriend 1.0 and a system conflict occurs, this can lead to a non-recoverable system crash. Some users have tried to download similar products such as Fling and 1NiteStand. Often, their systems have become infected with a virus. I recommend you keep Wife 1.0 and just deal with the situation. Having Wife 1.0 installed myself, I might also suggest you read the entire section regarding General Protection Faults (GPFs). You must assume all responsibility for faults and problems that might occur. The best course of action will be to push apologize button then reset button as soon as lock-up occurs. System will run smooth as long as you take the blame for all GPFs. Wife 1.0 is a great program but is very high maintenance. Suggestions for improved operation of Wife 1.0: Monthly use utilities such as TLC and FTD. Frequently use Communicator 5.0.

-Tech Support

WordPerfect Customer Support

A true story from a FORMER WordPerfect Customer Support employee from the WP Helpline.

Q: "Ridge Hall computer assistant; may I help you?"
A: "Yes, well, I'm having trouble with WordPerfect."

Q: "What sort of trouble?"
A: "Well, I was just typing along, and all of a sudden the words went away."

Q: "Went away?"
A: "They disappeared."

Q: "Hmmm. So, what does your screen look like now?"
A: "Nothing."

Q: "Nothing?"
A: "It's blank; it won't accept anything when I type."

Q: "Are you still in WordPerfect, or did you get out?"
A: "How do I tell?"

Q: "Can you see the C: prompt on the screen?"
A: "What's a C prompt?"

Q: "Never mind. Can you move the cursor around on the screen?"
A: "There isn't any cursor: I told you, it won't accept anything I type."

Q: "Does your monitor have a power indicator?"
A: "What's a monitor?"

Q: "It's the thing with the screen on it that looks like a TV. Does it have a little light that tells you when it's on?"
A: "I don't know."

Q: "Well, then look on the back of the monitor and find where the power cord goes into it. Can you see that?"
A: "Yes, I think so."

Q: "Great. Follow the cord to the plug, and tell me if it's plugged into the wall."
A: "Yes, it is."

Q: "When you were behind the monitor, did you notice that there were two cables plugged into the back of it, not just one?"
A: "No."

Q: "Well, there are -- I need you to look back there again and find the other cable."
A: "Okay, here it is."

Q: "Follow it for me, and tell me if it's plugged securely into the back of your computer."
A: "I can't reach."

Q: "Uh huh. Well, can you see if it is?"
A: "No."

Q: "Even if you maybe put your knee on something and lean way over?"
A: "Oh, it's not because I don't have the right angle; it's because it's dark."

Q: "Dark?"
A: "Yes, the office light is off, and the only light I have is coming in from the window."

Q: "Well, turn on the office light then."
A: "I can't."

Q: "No? Why not?"
A: "Because there's a power outage."

Q: "A power... A power outage? Aha, Okay, we've got it licked now. Do you still have the boxes and manuals and packing stuff your computer came in?"
A: "Well, yes, I keep them in the closet."

Q: "Good. Go get them, and unplug your system and pack it up just like it was when you got it. Then, take it back to the store you bought it from."
A: "Really? Is it that bad?"

Q: "Yes, I'm afraid it is."
A: "Well, all right then, I suppose. What do I tell them?"

Q: "Tell them you're too stupid to own a computer."

Famous Viruses

Lewinsky Virus:
Sucks all the memory out of your computer, then e-mails everyone about what it did.

Kenneth Starr Virus:
Completely examines every aspect of your computer then compiles a complex report that discredits every aspect of your computer.

Ronald Reagan Virus:
Saves your data, but forgets where it is stored.

Mike Tyson Virus:
Quits after two bytes. Spits everything out.

Oprah Winfrey Virus:
Your 300 MB hard drive suddenly shrinks to 100MB then slowly expands to 200 MB.

Dr. Jack Kevorkian Virus:
Deletes all old files.

Titanic Virus:
Your whole computer goes down.

Disney Virus:
Everything in your computer goes Goofy.

Prozac Virus:
Screws up your RAM but your processor doesn't care.

Joey Buttafuoco Virus:
Only attacks minor files.

Arnold Schwarzenegger Virus:
Terminates zome viles, leaves, but it vill be baaack.

Lorena Bobbit Virus:
Reformats your hard drive into a 3.5 inch floppy then discards it through Windows.

Viagra Virus:
Makes a new hard drive out of an old floppy.

Clinton Virus:
Gives you a 5" hard drive with no memory.

Real Stories Of The Non-technically Inclined

I worked with an individual who plugged his power strip back into itself and for the life of him could not understand why his computer would not turn on.

****

1st Person: "Do you know anything about this fax-machine?"
2nd Person: "A little. What's wrong?"
1st Person: "Well, I sent a fax, and the recipient called back to say all she received was a cover-sheet and a blank page. I tried it again, and the same thing happened."
2nd Person: "How did you load the sheet?"
1st Person: "It's a pretty sensitive memo, and I didn't want anyone else to read it by accident; so I folded it so only the recipient would open it and read it."

****

I recently saw a distraught young lady weeping beside her car. "Do you need help?" I asked. She replied, "I knew I should have replaced the battery in this remote door unlocker. Now, I can't get into my car. Do you think they (pointing to a distant convenience store) would have a battery for this?" "Hmmm, I dunno. Do you have an alarm too?" I asked. "No, just this remote 'thingy'," she answered, handing the car keys to me. As I took the key and manually unlocked the door, I replied, "Why don't you drive over there and check about the batteries . . . It's a long walk."

****

Tech Support: "What does the screen say now?"
Person: "It says, 'Hit enter when ready'."
Tech Support: "Well?"
Person: "How do I know when it's ready?"

****

My friend called his car insurance company to tell them to change his address from Texas to Vermont. The woman who took the call asked where Vermont was. As he tried to explain, she interrupted and said, "Look, I'm not stupid or anything, but what state is it in?"

****

Several years ago, we had an intern who was none too swift. One day, he was typing and turned to a secretary and said, "I'm almost out of typing paper. What do I do?" "Just use copier machine paper," she told him. With that, the intern took his last remaining blank piece of paper, put it in the photocopier and proceeded to make five blank copies.

****

I was working the help desk. One day, one of the computer operators called me and asked if anything "bad" would happen if she dropped coins into the openings of her PC. I asked if this was something she was thinking of doing. She said, "Never mind" and hung up. So, I got out my trusty tool kit and paid her a visit. I opened her CPU case and sure enough, there was 40 cents.

****

One of our servers crashed. I was watching our new system administrator trying to restore it. He inserted a CD and needed to type a path name to a directory named "i386." He started to type it and paused, asking me, "Where's the key for that line thing?" I asked what he was talking about, and he said, "You know, that one that looks like an upside-down exclamation mark." I replied, "You mean the letter "i?" and he said, "Yeah, that's it!"

****

This person had a broken lamp which he wanted to discard. Unfortunately, the power cord ran under his refrigerator, making it impossible to move the lamp while the cord was attached. He decided to cut the cord, since the lamp was unusable anyway, but didn't remember to unplug it first.

****

I was in a car dealership a while ago when a large motor home was towed into the garage. The front of the vehicle was in dire need of repair and the whole thing generally looked like an extra in "Twister." I asked the manager what had happened. He told me that the driver had set the cruise control, then went back to make a sandwich.

****

I called a company and asked to speak to Bob. The person who answered said, "Bob is on vacation. Would you like to hold?"

****

I rented a movie from Blockbuster. Before the movie begins, a message comes across the screen saying, "This movie has been altered to fit your television screen." Comment from my 15 year old daughter, "How do they know what size screen we have?"

Redneck Computer Terms

BACKUP:	What you do when you run across a skunk in the woods.
BAR CODE:	Them's the fight'n rules down at the local tavern.
BUG:	The reason you give for calling in sick.
BYTE:	What your pit bull dun to cusin Jethro.
CACHE:	Needed when you run out of food stamps.
CHIP:	Pasture muffins that you try not to step in.
TERMINAL:	Time to call the undertaker.
CRASH:	When you go to Junior's party uninvited.
DIGITAL:	The art of counting on your fingers.
DISKETTE:	Female Disco dancer.
FAX:	What you lie about to the IRS.
HACKER:	Uncle Leroy after 32 years of smoking.
HARDCOPY:	Picture looked at when selecting tattoos.
INTERNET:	Where cafeteria workers put their hair.
KEYBOARD:	Where you hang the keys to the John Deere.
MAC:	Big Bubba's favorite fast food.
MEGAHERTZ:	How your head feels after 17 beers.
MODEM:	What ya did when the grass and weeds got too tall.
MOUSE PAD:	Where Mickey and Minnie live.
NETWORK:	Scoop'n up a big fish before it breaks the line.
ONLINE:	Where to stay when taking the sobriety test.
ROM:	Where the pope lives.
SCREEN:	Helps keep the skeeters off the porch.
SERIAL PORT:	A red wine you drink with breakfast.
SUPERCONDUCTOR:	Amtrak's Employee of the year.
SCSI:	What you call your week-old underwear.

Cell Hand

A guy sitting at a bar shapes his hand like a telephone and starts talking into his hand. The bartender walks over and tells him this is a very tough neighborhood and he doesn't need any trouble here. The guy says, "You don't understand. I'm very hi-tech. I had a phone installed in my hand because I was tired of carrying around a cell phone." The bartender says, "Prove it." The guy dials up a number and hands his hand to the bartender. The bartender talks into the hand and carries on a conversation. "That's incredible," says the bartender. "I would never have believed it!" "Yeah," said the guy, "I can keep in touch with my broker, my wife, you name it. By the way, where is the men's room?" The bartender directs him to the men's room. The guy goes in and 5, 10, 20 minutes go by and he doesn't return. Fearing the worst given the neighborhood, the bartender goes into the men's room. There is the guy spread-eagle on the wall. His pants are around his ankles and he has toilet paper hanging from his butt. "Oh my!" says the bartender. "Did they rob you? Are you hurt?" The guy turns and says, "No, I'm ok. I'm just waiting for a fax."

A Little Poem Regarding Computer Spell Checkers
(Try running this through your spell checker.)

Eye halve a spelling chequer
It came with my pea sea
It plainly marques four my revue
Miss steaks eye kin knot sea.

Eye strike a key and type a word
And weight four it two say
Weather eye am wrong oar write
It shows me strait a weigh.

As soon as a mist ache is maid
It nose bee fore two long
And eye can put the error rite
Its rare lea ever wrong.

Eye have run this poem threw it
I am shore your pleased two no
Its letter perfect awl the weigh
My chequer tolled me sew.

Y2K Update

"The IT staff has completed the 3 years of work on time and on budget. We have gone through every line of code in every program in every system. We have analyzed all databases, all data files, including backups and historic archives, and modified all data to reflect the change. We are proud to report that we have completed the "Y-to-K" date change mission, and have now implemented all changes to all programs and all data to reflect the following new standards: Januark, Februark, March, April, Mak, June, Julk, August, September, October, November, December and...Sundak, Mondak, Tuesdak, Wednesdak, Thursdak, Fridak, Saturdak. We trust that this is satisfactory, because to be honest, none of this Y to K problem has made any sense to us. But, we understand it is a global problem, and our team is glad to help in any way possible. And, what does the year 2000 have to do with it? Speaking of which, what do you think we ought to do next year when the two digit year rolls over from 99 to 00? We'll await your direction."

The Gender Of Computers

A pastor of one church who was previously a sailor, was very aware that ships are addressed as "she" and "her." He often wondered what gender computers should be addressed. To answer that question, he set up two groups of computer experts. The first was comprised of women, and the second of men. Each group was asked to recommend whether computers should be referred to in the feminine gender or the masculine gender. They were asked to give 4 reasons for their recommendation.

The group of women reported that the computers should be referred to in the masculine gender because:
1. In order to get their attention, you have to turn them on.
2. They have a lot of data, but are still clueless.
3. They are supposed to help you solve problems, but half the time they are the problem.
4. As soon as you commit to one, you realize that, if you had waited a little longer you could have had a better one.

The men, on the other hand concluded that computers should be referred to in the feminine gender because:
1. No one but the Creator understands their internal logic.
2. The native language they use to communicate with other computers is incomprehensible to everyone else.
3. Even your smallest mistakes are stored in long-term memory for retrieval.
4. As soon as you make a commitment to one, you find yourself spending half your paycheck on accessories for it.

Mouse Balls Memo

MEMO: Mouse Balls

Mouse balls are now available as FRU (Field Replacement Unit). Therefore, if a mouse fails to operate or should it perform erratically, it may need a ball replacement. Because of the delicate nature of this procedure, replacement of mouse balls should only be attempted by properly trained personnel. Before proceeding, determine the type of mouse balls by examining the underside of the mouse. Domestic balls will be larger and harder than foreign balls. Ball removal procedures differ depending upon the manufacturer of the mouse. Foreign balls can be replaced using the pop-off method. Domestic balls are replaced by using the twist-off method. Mouse balls are not usually static-sensitive. However, excessive handling can result in sudden discharge. Upon completion of ball replacement, the mouse may be used immediately. It is recommended that each replacer have a pair of spare balls for maintaining optimum customer satisfaction. Any customer missing his balls should suspect local personnel of removing these necessary items.

"CRAZY TIMES" VIRUS WARNING

Folks, I don't normally send out virus warnings, but this one is extremely serious. Please read very carefully and take care! If you receive an email entitled "Crazy Times" delete it immediately. Do not open it! Apparently this one is pretty nasty. It will not only erase everything on your hard drive, but it will also delete anything on disks within 20 feet of your computer. It demagnetizes the stripes on ALL of your credit cards. It reprograms your ATM PIN number, messes up the tracking on your DVD player and uses subspace field harmonics to scratch any CD's you attempt to play. It will re-calibrate your refrigerator's coolness settings so all your ice cream melts and your milk curdles. It will program your phone autodial to call only your mother-in-law's number. This virus will mix antifreeze into your fish tank. It will drink all your beer. It will leave dirty socks on the coffee table when you are expecting company. Its radioactive emissions will cause your toe jam and bellybutton fuzz to migrate behind your ears. It will replace your shampoo with Nair and your Nair with Rogaine, all while dating your current boy/girlfriend behind your back and billing their hotel rendezvous to your Visa card. It will cause you to run with scissors and throw things in a way that is only fun until someone loses an eye. It will give you Dutch Elm Disease and Tinea. It will rewrite your backup files, changing all your active verbs to passive tense and incorporating undetectable misspellings which grossly change the interpretations of key sentences. If the "Crazy Times" message is opened in a Windows 8 environment, it will leave the toilet seat up and leave your hair dryer plugged in dangerously close to a full bathtub. It will not only remove the tags from your mattresses and pillows, but it will also refill your skimmed milk with whole milk. It will replace all your luncheon meat with Spam. It will molecularly rearrange your cologne or perfume, causing it to smell like dill pickles. It is insidious and subtle. It is dangerous and terrifying to behold. It is also a rather interesting shade of mauve. These are just a few signs of infection.

PLEASE FORWARD THIS MESSAGE TO EVERYONE YOU KNOW!!!

Thanks to Bill Gates and a small child with kidney failure for sending that in. If you pass this to at least 5 friends within the next three minutes Bill will give the kid a free copy of Windows 8.

The Polygraph Test

Police in Radnor, Pennsylvania interrogated a suspect by placing a metal colander on his head and connecting it with wires to a photocopy machine. The message "He's lying!" was placed in the copier, and police pressed the copy button each time they thought the suspect wasn't telling the truth. Believing the "lie detector" was working, the suspect confessed.

Subject: Y(0)

Translated from Latin scroll dated 2BC

Dear Cassius,

Are you still working on the Y (zero) problem? This change from BC to AD is giving us a lot of headaches and we haven't much time left. I don't know how people will cope with working the wrong way around. Having been working happily downwards forever, now we have to start thinking upwards. You would think that someone would have thought of it earlier and not left it to us to sort it all out at this last minute. I spoke to Caesar Augustus the other evening. He was livid that Julius hadn't done something about it when he was sorting out the calendar. He said he could see why Brutus turned nasty. We called in Consultus, but he simply said that continuing downwards using minus BC won't work and as usual charged a fortune for doing nothing useful. Surely, we will not have to throw out all our hardware and start again? Macrohard will make yet another fortune out of this, I suppose. The money lenders are paranoid of course! They have been told that all usury rates will invert and they will have to pay their clients to take out loans. It's an ill wind. As for myself, I just can't see the sand in an hourglass flowing upwards. We have heard that there are three wise men in the East who have been working on the problem, but unfortunately they won't arrive until it's all over. I have heard that there are plans to stable all horses at midnight at the turn of the year as there are fears that they will stop and try to run backwards, causing immense damage to chariots and possible loss of life. Some say the world will cease to exist at the moment of transition. Anyway, we are still continuing to work on this blasted Y(0) problem. I will send a parchment to you if anything further develops. If you have any ideas please let me know.

Plutonius

The Computer Industry vs. The Auto Industry

At a recent computer expo (COMDEX), Bill Gates reportedly compared the computer industry with the auto industry and stated, "If GM had kept up with technology like the computer industry has, we would all be driving twenty-five dollar cars that got 1000 mi/gal."

Recently, General Motors addressed this comment by releasing the statement: "Yes, but would you want your car to crash twice a day?"

IF MICROSOFT BUILT CARS....

1. Every time they repainted the lines on the road you would have to buy a new car.

2. Occasionally, your car would die on the freeway for no reason, and you would just accept this, restart and drive on.

3. Occasionally, executing a maneuver would cause your car to stop and fail and you would have to re-install the engine. For some strange reason, you would accept this too.

4. You could only have one person in the car at a time, unless you bought "Car95" or "CarNT." But, then you would have to buy more seats.

5. Macintosh would make a car that was powered by the sun, was reliable, five times as fast, twice as easy to drive - but would only run on 5 percent of the roads.

6. The Macintosh car owners would get expensive Microsoft upgrades to their cars, which would make their cars run much slower.

7. The oil, gas, and alternator warning lights would be replaced by a single "general car default" warning light.

8. New seats would force everyone to have the same size butt.

9. The airbag system would say "are you sure?" before going off.

10. If you were involved in a crash, you would have no idea what happened.

<u>Minnesota Guide To Computer Lingo</u>

LOG ON: making da vood stove hotter
LOG OFF: don't add vood
MONITOR :   keep an eye on da vood stove
MEGAHERTZ: vhen a big log drops on your barefoot in da morning
FLOPPY DISK: vhat you get from piling too much vood
RAM: da hydraulic ting dat makes da voodsplitter vork
DRIVE: getting home during most of da vinter
PROMPT: vhat ya vish da mail vas during da snow season
ENTER: come on in
WINDOWS: vhat ya shut vhen it gets 10 below
SCREEN: vhat is a must during black fly season
CHIP: vhat ya munch during Vikings games
MICROCHIP: vhat's left in da bag vhen da chips are gone
MODEM: vhat ya did to da hay fields last Yuly
DOT MATRIX: Eino Matrix's wife
LAPTOP: vhere da grandkids sit
KEYBOARD: vhere ya suppose to put da keys so da Misses can find em
SOFTWARE: da plastic picnic utensils, ya? or vhat da li'l vomen likes
MOUSE: vhat leaves dem little turds in da cupboard
MAINFRAME: da part of da sauna that holds up da roof
PORT: vhere da commericial fishin boats dock
RANDOM ACCESS MEMORY: vhen ya can't remember how much ya spent on
da new deer rifle vhen da wife asks about it

Credit Card Chaos

In March, 1992, a man living in Newtown near Boston Massachusetts received a bill for his as yet unused credit card stating that he owed $0.00. He ignored it and threw it away. In April, he received another and threw that one away too. The following month the credit card company sent him a very nasty note stating they were going to cancel his card if he didn't send them $0.00 by return of post. He called them, talked to them, they said it was a computer error, and told him they'd take care of it. The following month he decided that it was about time that he tried out the trouble-some credit card figuring that if there were purchases on his account it would put an end to his ridiculous predicament. However, in the first store that he produced his credit card in payment for his purchases he found that his card had been canceled. He called the credit card company who apologized for the computer error once again and said that they would take care of it.

The next day, he got a bill for $0.00 stating that payment was now overdue. Assuming that having spoken to the credit card company only the previous day, the latest bill was yet another mistake he ignored it, trusting that the company would be as good as their word and sort the problem out. The next month, he got a bill for $0.00 stating that he had 10 days to pay his account or the company would have to take steps to recover the debt. Finally giving in, he thought he would play the company at their own game and mailed them a check for $0.00. The computer duly processed his account and returned a statement to the effect that he now owed the credit card company nothing at all. A week later, the man's bank called him asking him what he was doing writing a check for $0.00. After a lengthy explanation, the bank replied that the $0.00 check had caused their check processing software to fail. The bank could not now process ANY checks from ANY of their customers that day because the check for $0.00 was causing the computer to crash. The following month, the man received a letter from the credit card company claiming that his check had bounced and that he now owed them $0.00 and unless he sent a check by return of post they would be taking steps to recover the debt. The man, who had been considering buying his wife a computer for her birthday, bought her a typewriter instead.

An Email Parody

I know this guy whose neighbor, a young man, was home recovering from having been served a rat in his bucket of Kentucky Fried Chicken. So anyway, one day he went to sleep and when he awoke he was in his bathtub and it was full of ice and he was sore all over. When he got out of the tub he realized that HIS KIDNEY HAD BEEN STOLEN and he saw a note on his mirror that said, "Call 911!" But, he was afraid to use his phone because it was connected to his computer, and there was a virus on his computer that would destroy his hard drive if he opened an e-mail entitled "Join the crew!" He knew it wasn't a hoax because he himself was a computer programmer who was working on software to save us from Armageddon when the year 2000 rolls around. His program will prevent a global disaster in which all the computers get together and distribute the $600 Nieman Marcus cookie recipe under the leadership of Bill Gates. (It's true-I read it all last week in a mass e-mail from BILL GATES HIMSELF, who was also promising me a free MacBook and $5,000 if I would forward the e-mail to everyone I know.) The poor man then tried to call 911 from a pay phone to report his missing kidney, but reaching into the coin-return slot he got jabbed with an HIV-infected needle around which was wrapped a note that said, "Welcome to the world of AIDS." Luckily he was only a few blocks from the hospital - the one, actually, where that little boy who is dying of cancer is, the one whose last wish is for everyone in the world to send him an e-mail and the American Cancer Society has agreed to pay him a nickel for every e-mail he receives. I sent him two e-mails and one of them was a bunch of x's and o's in the shape of an angel (if you get it and forward it to twenty people you will have good luck, ten people you will only have OK luck, and if you send it to less than ten people you will have BAD LUCK FOR SEVEN YEARS). So, anyway the poor guy tried to drive himself to the hospital, but on the way he noticed another car driving along without his lights on. To be helpful, he flashed his lights at him and was promptly shot as part of a gang initiation. And, it's a little-known fact that the Y1K problem caused the Dark Ages.

Boyle's Law

Reportedly, a true story.....

A thermodynamics professor wrote a take home exam for his graduate students. It had one question: Is hell exothermic or endothermic? Support your answer with a proof. Most of the students wrote proofs of their beliefs using Boyle's Law or some variant. One student, however, wrote the following.....

First, we must postulate that if souls exist, then they must have some mass. If they do, then a mole of souls can also have a mass. So, at what rate are souls moving into hell and at what rate are souls leaving? I think that we can safely assume that once a soul gets to hell, it will not leave. Therefore, no souls are leaving. As for souls entering hell, let's look at the different religions that exist in the world today. Some of these religions state that if you are not a member of their religion, you will go to hell. Since there are more than one of these religions and people do not belong to more than one religion, we can project that all people and all souls go to hell.

With birth and death rates as they are, we can expect the number of souls in hell to increase exponentially. Now, we look at the rate of change in volume in hell. Boyle's Law states that in order for the temperature and pressure in hell to stay the same, the ratio of the mass of souls and volume needs to stay constant.

1. So, if hell is expanding at a slower rate than the rate at which souls enter hell, then the temperature and pressure in hell will increase until all hell breaks loose.
2. Of course, if hell is expanding at a rate faster than the increase of souls in hell, then the temperature and pressure will drop until hell freezes over.

So which is it? If we accept the postulate given to me by Therese Banyan during Freshman year, "that it will be a cold night in hell before I sleep with you" and take into account the fact that I still have not succeeded in having sexual relations with her, then #2 cannot be true, and hell is exothermic.

The student got the only A.

Understanding Engineers

Part One:

An architect, an artist and an engineer were discussing whether it was better to spend time with the wife or a mistress. The architect said he enjoyed time with his wife, building a solid foundation for an enduring relationship. The artist said he enjoyed time with his mistress, because of the passion and mystery he found there. The engineer said, "I like both." "Both?" wondered the artist. "Yeah," said the engineer. "If you have a wife and a mistress, they will each assume you are spending time with the other woman, and you can go to the plant and get some work done."

Part Two:

To the optimist, the glass is half full. To the pessimist, the glass is half empty. To the engineer, the glass is twice as big as it needs to be.

Part Three:

Q: What is the difference between Mechanical Engineers and Civil Engineers?
A: Mechanical Engineers build weapons -- Civil Engineers build targets.

Part Four:

The graduate with a Science degree asks, "Why does it work?" The graduate with an Engineering degree asks, "How does it work?" The graduate with an Accounting degree asks, "How much will it cost?" The graduate with an Arts degree asks, "Do you want fries with that?"

Part Five:

Two engineers were walking across campus when one said to the other, "Where did you get such a great looking bike?" The second engineer replied, "Well, I was just strolling along yesterday minding my own business when a beautiful well-built woman rode up on this bike. She threw the bike to the ground, took off all her clothes, exposing a milky-white firm body. In a soft whisper, she said, 'Take what you want'." The second engineer nodded approvingly, "Good choice! Her clothes probably wouldn't have fit."

J.D. Heskin

Things To Think About

The Value Of A Smile

She smiled at a sorrowful stranger.
The smile seemed to make him feel better.
He remembered past kindness of a friend,
And wrote him a thank you letter.

The friend was so pleased with the thank you
That he left a large tip after lunch.
The waitress, surprised by the size of the tip,
Bet the whole thing on a hunch.

The next day, she picked up her winnings
And gave part to a man on the street.
The man on the street was grateful;
For two days he'd had nothing to eat.

After he finished his dinner,
He left for his small dingy room.
He didn't know at that moment
That he might be facing his doom.

On the way he picked up a shivering puppy
And took him home to get warm.
The puppy was very grateful
To be in out of the storm.

That night the house caught on fire.
The puppy barked the alarm.
He barked till he woke the whole household
And saved everybody from harm.

One of the boys that he rescued
Grew up to be President.
All this because of a simple smile
That hadn't cost a cent.

A Perfect Little Angel

I had offered to watch my 3-year-old daughter, Nicole, so that my wife could go out with a friend. I was getting some work done while Nicole appeared to be having a good time in the other room. No problem, I figured. But, then it got a little too quiet and I yelled out, "What are you doing, Nicole?" No response. I repeated my question and heard her say, "Oh...nothing." Nothing? What does "nothing" mean? I got up from my desk and ran out into the living room, whereupon I saw her take off down the hall. I chased her up the stairs and watched her as her little behind made a hard left into the bedroom. I was gaining on her! She took off for the bathroom. Bad move. I had her cornered. I told her to turn around. She refused.

I pulled out my big, mean, authoritative Daddy voice, "Young lady, I said turn around!" Slowly, she turned toward me. In her hand was what was left of my wife's new lipstick. And, every square inch of her face was covered with bright red (except her lips of course)! As she looked up at me with fearful eyes, lips trembling, I heard every voice that had been shouted to me as a child. "How could you...You should know better than that...How many times have you been told...What a bad thing to do..." It was just a matter of my picking out which old message I was going to use on her so that she would know what a bad girl she had been. But, before I could let loose, I looked down at the sweatshirt my wife had put on her only an hour before. In big letters it said, "I'M A PERFECT LITTLE ANGEL!" I looked back up into her tearful eyes and instead of seeing a bad girl who didn't listen, I saw a child of God...a perfect little angel full of worth, value and a wonderful spontaneity that I had come dangerously close to shaming out of her. "Sweetheart, you look beautiful! Let's take a picture so Mommy can see how special you look." I took the picture and thanked God that I didn't miss the opportunity to reaffirm what a perfect little angel He had given me.

A Gink

The other night my three year old son and I had been through the regular nightly routine: story, prayer, hugs. Then, as my hand slid down the light switch, "I want a gink." He can't say "drink" and I thought it was kinda' cute, "gink." But, I was firm. "You just had a drink when you brushed your teeth. Now it is time to go to sleep." At last the kids were all in bed. Peace. Silence. I sat in the best chair and began to sort through the mail. "I want a gink!" from the darkness. "Gink" lost some of it's cuteness. "No water! Go to sleep." Quietness reigned for at least 60 seconds. "Daddy, I want a gink." "Be quiet." "I want a gink." I knew how Moses felt in the wilderness with a million Jews all crying, "We want a gink." Gink was no longer cute. I yelled down the hallway into the darkness, "If I hear you ask for a gink one more time, if I hear one sound from you, I'm gonna come down there and spank you and I'm not kidding. Now be quiet and go to sleep." It was as quiet as a tomb, not a sound. You could have heard a pin drop. It was so silent I couldn't concentrate on the mail. Then, the still small voice of a child who smelled victory. "Daddy, when you come in here to spank me could you bring me a gink of water?" You can't keep a good man down!

Instructions For Life

1. Give people more than they expect and do it cheerfully.
2. Memorize your favorite poem.
3. Don't believe all you hear, spend all you have, or sleep all you want.
4. When you say, "I love you," mean it.
5. When you say, "I'm sorry," look the person in the eye.
6. Be engaged at least six months before you get married.
7. Believe in love at first sight.
8. Never laugh at anyone's dreams. People who don't have dreams don't have much.
9. Love deeply and passionately. You might get hurt but it's the only way to live life completely.
10. In disagreements, fight fairly. No name calling.
11. Don't judge people by their relatives.
12. Talk slowly but think quickly.
13. When someone asks you a question you don't want to answer, smile and ask, "Why do you want to know?"
14. Remember that great love and great achievements involve great risk.
15. Call your mom.
16. Say "God bless you" when you hear someone sneeze.
17. When you lose, don't lose the lesson.
18. Remember the 3 R's: Respect for self; Respect for others; Responsibility for all your actions.
19. Don't let a little dispute injure a great friendship.
20. When you realize you've made a mistake, take immediate steps to correct it.
21. Smile when picking up the phone. The caller will hear it in your voice.
22. Marry a man/woman you love to talk to. As you get older, their conversational skills will be as important as any other quality.
23. Spend some time alone.
24. Open your arms to change, but don't let go of your values.
25. Remember that silence is sometimes the best answer.
26. Read more books and watch less TV.
27. Live an honorable life, so when you get old and think back, you'll get to enjoy it a 2nd time.
28. Trust in God but lock your car.
29. Do all you can to create a tranquil, harmonious home.
30. In disagreements with loved ones, deal with the current situation. Don't bring up the past.
31. Read between the lines.
32. Share your knowledge. It's a way to achieve immortality.
33. Be gentle with the earth.
34. Pray. There's immeasurable power in it.
35. Never interrupt when you are being flattered.
36. Mind your own business.
37. Don't trust a man/woman who doesn't close his/her eyes when you kiss.
38. Once a year, go someplace you've never been before.
39. If you make a lot of money, put it to use helping others while you are living.

40. Remember that not getting what you want is sometimes a stroke of luck.
41. Learn the rules, then break some.
42. Remember that the best relationship is one where your love for each other is greater than your need for each other.
43. Judge your success by what you had to give up in order to get it.
44. Remember that your character is your destiny.
45. Approach love and cooking with reckless abandon.

God's Job (A Child's View)

One of God's main jobs is making people. He makes them to replace the ones that die so there will be enough people to take care of things here on earth. He doesn't make grown-ups, just babies. I think because they are smaller and easier to make. That way, He doesn't have to take up His valuable time teaching them to talk and walk. He can just leave that to the mothers and fathers. God's second most important job is listening to prayers. An awful lot of this goes on, since some people, like preachers and things, pray at times besides bedtime. God doesn't have time to listen to the radio or TV on account of this. Since He hears everything, not only prayers, there must be a terrible lot of noise in His ears, unless He has thought of a way to turn it off. God sees everything and hears everything and is everywhere, which keeps Him pretty busy. So, you shouldn't go wasting His time by going over your parent's head asking for something they said you couldn't have.

Atheists are people who don't believe in God. I don't think there are any in Duluth. At least there aren't any who come to our church. Jesus is God's son. He used to do all the hard work like walking on water and performing miracles and trying to teach the people who didn't want to learn about God. They finally got tired of Him preaching to them and they crucified Him. But, He was good and kind like His Father and He told His Father that they didn't know what they were doing and to forgive them and God said, "OK." His dad (God) appreciated everything that He had done and all His hard work on earth so He told Him He didn't have to go out on the road anymore. He could stay in heaven. So, He did. And, now He helps His Dad out by listening to prayers and seeing things which are important for God to take care of and which ones He can take care of Himself without having to bother God. Like a secretary, only more important, of course. You can pray anytime you want and they are sure to hear you because they got it worked out so one of them is on duty all the time.

You should always go to Church on Sunday because it makes God happy, and if there's anybody you want to make happy, it's God. Don't skip church to do something you think will be more fun like going to the beach. This is wrong! And, besides, the sun doesn't come out at the beach until noon anyway. If you don't believe in God, besides being an atheist, you will be very lonely, because your parents can't go everywhere with you, like to camp, but God can. It is good to know He's around you when you're scared in the dark or when you can't swim very good and you get thrown into real deep water by big kids. But, you shouldn't just always think of what God can do for you. I figure God put me here and He can take me back anytime He pleases.

A Little Boy With A Bad Temper

There was a little boy with a bad temper and a foul mouth that he inflicted on family and friends alike. His father gave him a bag of nails and told him that every time he lost his temper, he should hammer a nail into the back fence. The first day, the boy had driven 37 nails into the fence. Then, it gradually dwindled down. He discovered it was easier to hold his temper than to drive those nails into the fence. Finally, the day came when the boy didn't lose his temper at all. He told his father about it and the father suggested that the boy now pull out one nail for each day that he was able to hold his temper. The days passed and the young boy was finally able to tell his father that all the nails were gone. The father took his son by the hand and led him to the fence. He said, "You have done well, my son, but look at the holes in the fence. The fence will never be the same. When you say things in anger, they leave a scar just like this one. You can put a knife in a man, draw it out, and it won't matter how many times you say, "I'm sorry;" the wound is still there. A verbal wound is as bad as a physical one. Friends are a very rare jewel, indeed. They make you smile and encourage you to succeed. They lend an ear, they share a word of praise, and they always want to open their hearts to us. Show your friends how much you care and save your anger for hammering nails.

The Shape Women Are In

Did you know....

If shop mannequins were real women, THEY'D BE TOO THIN TO MENSTRUATE?

There are 3 billion women who don't look like supermodels and ONLY 8 WHO DO.

Marilyn Monroe wore a SIZE 12.

If Barbie was a real woman, she'd have to walk on all fours due to her proportions.

The average American woman weighs 144 lbs. and wears between a size 12 and 14.

One out of every 4 college aged women has an eating disorder.

The models in the magazines are airbrushed-THEY'RE NOT PERFECT!!

A psychological study in 1995 found that 3 minutes spent looking at models in a fashion magazine caused 70% of women to feel depressed, guilty and shameful.

Models twenty years ago weighed 8% less than the average woman, today models weigh 23% less.

<u>You Are My Sunshine</u>

Like any good mother, when Karen found out that another baby was on the way, she did what she could to help her 3 year old son, Michael, prepare for a new sibling. They found out that the new baby was going to be a girl, and day after day, night after night, Michael sang to his sister in Mommy's tummy. The pregnancy progressed normally for Karen. Then, the labor pains came. Every five minutes.....every minute. But, complications arose during delivery. Hours of labor. Would a c-section be required? Finally, Michael's little sister was born. But, she was in serious condition. With sirens howling in the night, the ambulance rushed the infant to the neonatal intensive care unit.

The days inched by and the little girl got worse. The pediatric specialist told the parents, "There is very little hope. Be prepared for the worst." Karen and her husband contacted a local cemetery about a burial plot. They fixed up a special room in their home for the new baby and now they were planning a funeral. Michael kept begging his parents to let him see his sister. "I want to sing to her," he said. Week two in intensive care, it looked as if a funeral would come before the week is over. Michael kept nagging about singing to his sister but kids are never allowed in Intensive Care. But, Karen made up her mind. She would take Michael whether they like it or not. "If he doesn't see his sister now, he may never see her alive." She dressed him in an oversized scrub suit and marches him into ICU. He looked like a walking laundry basket, but the head nurse recognized him as a child and bellowed, "Get that kid out of here now! No children are allowed!" The mother rose up strong in Karen, and the usually mild-mannered lady glared steel-eyed into the head nurse's face, her lips a firm line. "He is not leaving until he sings to his sister!"

Karen towed Michael to his sister's bedside. He gazed at the tiny infant losing the battle to live, and began to sing. In the pure hearted voice of a 3 year old, Michael sang, "You are my sunshine, my only sunshine, you make me happy when skies are gray…" Instantly, the baby girl responded. The pulse rate became calm and steady. "Keep on singing, Michael." "You never know, dear, how much I love you. Please don't take my sunshine away…" The ragged, strained breathing became as smooth as a kitten's purr. "Keep on singing, Michael." "The other night, dear, as I lay sleeping, I dreamed I held you in my arms…" Michael's little sister relaxed as rest, healing rest, seemed to sweep over her. "Keep on singing, Michael." Tears conquered the face of the bossy head nurse. Karen glowed. "You are my sunshine, my only sunshine. Please don't take my sunshine away." Funeral plans were scrapped. The next day…the very next day, the little girl was well enough to go home! A national woman's magazine called it "the miracle of a brother's song." The medical staff just called it a miracle. Karen called it a miracle of God's love!

Email This!

Fun Facts

Coca-Cola was originally green.

Every day more money is printed for Monopoly than the US Treasury.

It is possible to lead a cow upstairs but not downstairs.

Smartest dogs: 1) Scottish border collie; 2) Poodle; 3) Golden retriever.
Dumbest: Afghan hound.

Hawaiian alphabet has 12 letters.

Men can read smaller print than women; women can hear better.

Amount American Airlines dollars saved in 1987 by eliminating one olive from each salad served first class: $40,000

City with the most Rolls Royce's per capita: Hong Kong

State with the highest percentage of people who walk to work: Alaska

Percentage of Africa that is wilderness: 28%

Percentage of North America that is wilderness: 38%

Barbie's measurements if she were life size: 39-23-33

Average number of days a German goes without washing his underwear: 7

Percentage of American men who say they would marry the same woman if they had it to do all over again: 80%

Percentage of American women who say they'd marry the same man: 50%

Cost of raising a medium-size dog to the age of eleven: $6,400

Average number of people airborne over the US any given hour: 61,000.

Percentage of Americans who have visited Disneyland/Disney World: 70%

Average life span of a major league baseball: 7 pitches.

Only President to win a Pulitzer: John F. Kennedy for Profiles in Courage.

Intelligent people have more zinc and copper in their hair.

The world's youngest parents were 8 and 9 and lived in China in 1910.

The youngest pope was 11 years old.

Iceland consumes more Coca-Cola per capita than any other nation.

First novel ever written on a typewriter: Tom Sawyer.

A duck's quack doesn't echo, and no one knows why.

In the 1940s, the FCC assigned television's Channel 1 to mobile services (two-way radios in taxicabs, for instance) but did not re-number the other channel assignments. That is why your TV set has channels 2 and up, but no channel 1.

The San Francisco Cable cars are the only mobile National Monuments.

The only 15 letter word that can be spelled without repeating a letter is uncopyrightable.

"Hang On Sloopy" is the official rock song of Ohio.

Did you know that there are coffee flavored PEZ?

The reason firehouses have circular stairways is from the days of yore when the engines were pulled by horses. The horses were stabled on the ground floor and figured out how to walk up straight staircases.

The airplane Buddy Holly died in was the "American Pie." (Thus the name of the Don McLean song.)

When opossums are playing 'possum, they are not "playing." They actually pass out from sheer terror.

The Main Library at Indiana University sinks over an inch every year because when it was built, engineers failed to take into account the weight of all the books that would occupy the building.

Each king in a deck of playing cards represents a great king from history.
Spades - King David, Clubs - Alexander the Great,
Hearts - Charlemagne, and Diamonds - Julius Caesar.

111,111,111 x 111,111,111 = 12,345,678,987,654,321

If a statue in the park of a person on a horse has both front legs in the air, the person died in battle; if the horse has one front leg in the air, the person died as a result of wounds received in battle; if the horse has all four legs on the ground, the person died of natural causes.

Clans of long ago that wanted to get rid of their unwanted people without killing them would burn their houses down - hence the expression "to get fired."

Only two people signed the Declaration of Independence on July 4th, John Hancock and Charles Thomson. Most of the rest signed on August 2, but the last signature wasn't added until 5 years later.

"I am." is the shortest complete sentence in the English language.

The term "the whole 9 yards" came from W.W.II fighter pilots in the South Pacific. When arming their airplanes on the ground, the .50 caliber machine gun ammo belts measured exactly 27 feet, before being loaded into the fuselage. If the pilots fired all their ammo at a target, it got "the whole 9 yards."

Hershey's Kisses are called that because the machine that makes them looks like it's kissing the conveyor belt.

The phrase "rule of thumb" is derived from an old English law which stated that you couldn't beat your wife with anything wider than your thumb.

An ostrich's eye is bigger that it's brain.

The longest recorded flight of a chicken is thirteen seconds.

The Eisenhower interstate system requires that one mile in every five must be straight. These straight sections are usable as airstrips in times of war or other emergencies.

In every episode of Seinfeld there is a Superman somewhere.

The name Jeep came from the abbreviation used in the army for the "General Purpose" vehicle, G.P.

The Pentagon, in Arlington, Virginia, has twice as many bathrooms as is necessary. When it was built in the 1940s, the state of Virginia still had segregation laws requiring separate toilet facilities for blacks and whites.

The cruise liner, Queen Elizabeth II, moves only six inches for each gallon of diesel that it burns.

The highest point in Pennsylvania is lower than the lowest point in Colorado.

Nutmeg is extremely poisonous if injected intravenously.

If you have three quarters, four dimes, and four pennies, you have $1.19. You also have the largest amount of money in coins without being able to make change for a dollar.

The first toilet ever seen on television was on "Leave It To Beaver."

The only two days of the year in which there are no professional sports games (MLB, NBA, NHL, or NFL) are the day before and the day after the Major League all-stars Game.

Only one person in two billion will live to be 116 or older.

The name Wendy was made up for the book "Peter Pan."

<u>**Things I've Learned**</u>

I've learned that you can't hide a piece of broccoli in a glass of milk. Age 7

I've learned that I like my teacher because she cries when we sing "Silent Night." Age 7

I've learned that when I wave to people in the country, they stop what they are doing and wave back. Age 9

I've learned that just when I get my room the way I like it, Mom makes me clean it up. Age 13

I've learned that if you want to cheer yourself up, you should try cheering someone else up. Age 13

I've learned that although it's hard to admit it, I'm secretly glad my parents are strict with me. Age 15

I've learned that silent company is often more healing than words of advice. Age 24

I've learned that brushing my child's hair is one of life's great leisures. Age 29

I've learned that wherever I go, the world's worst drivers have followed me there. Age 29

I've learned that if someone says something unkind about me, I must live so that no one will believe it. Age 39

I've learned that there are people who love you dearly but just don't know how to show it. Age 41

I've learned that you can make someone's day by simply send them a little card. Age 44

I've learned that children and grandparents are natural allies. Age 46

I've learned that the greater a person's sense of guilt, the greater his need to cast blame on others. Age 46

I've learned that singing "Amazing Grace" can lift my spirits for hours. Age 49

I've learned that motel mattresses are better on the side away from the phone. Age 50

I've learned that you can tell a lot about a man by the way he handles these three things: a rainy day, lost luggage, and tangled Christmas tree lights. Age 52

I've learned that regardless of your relationship with your parents, you miss them terribly after they die. Age 53

I've learned that making a living is not the same thing as making a life. Age 58

I've learned that if you want to do something positive for your children, try to improve your marriage. Age 61

I've learned that life sometimes gives you a second chance. Age 62

I've learned that you shouldn't go through life with a catcher's mitt on both hands. You need to be able to throw something back. Age 64

I've learned that if you pursue happiness, it will elude you. However, if you focus on your family, the needs of others, your work, meeting new people, and doing the very best you can, happiness will find you. Age 65

I've learned that whenever I decide something with kindness, I usually make the right decision. Age 66

I've learned that everyone can use a prayer. Age 72

I've learned that it pays to believe in miracles. To tell the truth, I've seen several. Age 73

I've learned that every day you should reach out and touch someone. People love that human touch - holding hands, a warm hug, or just a friendly pat on the back. Age 85

I've learned that I still have a lot to learn. Age 92

Handy Tips For Life

1. Stuff a miniature marshmallow in the bottom of a sugar cone to prevent ice cream drip.

2. Use a meat baster to "squeeze" your pancake batter onto the hot griddle for perfect shaped pancakes every time.

3. To keep potatoes from budding, place an apple in the bag with the potatoes.

4. To prevent egg shells from cracking, add a pinch of salt to the water before hard-boiling

5. Run your hands under cold water before pressing Rice Krispies treats in the pan and the marshmallow won't stick to your fingers.

6. To get the most juice out of fresh lemons, bring them to room temperature and roll them under your palm against the kitchen counter before squeezing.

7. To easily remove burnt-on food from your skillet, simply add a drop or two of dish soap and enough water to cover bottom of pan, and bring to a boil on stove-top and the skillet will be much easier to clean now

8. Spray your Tupperware with nonstick cooking spray before pouring in tomato-based sauces and you'll have no more stains.

9. When a cake recipe calls for flouring the baking pan, use a bit of the dry cake mix instead, so you'll have no white mess on the outside of the cake.

10. If you accidentally over-salt a dish while it's still cooking, drop in a peeled potato because it absorbs the excess salt for an instant "fix me up."

11. Wrap celery in aluminum foil when putting in the refrigerator and it will keep for weeks.

12. Brush beaten egg white over pie crust before baking to yield a beautiful glossy finish.

13. Place a slice of apple in hardened brown sugar to soften it backup.

14. When boiling corn on the cob, add a pinch of sugar to help bring out the corns natural sweetness.

15. To determine whether an egg is fresh, immerse it in a pan of cool, salted water. If it sinks, it is fresh and if it rises to the surface, throw it away.

16. Cure for headaches: Take a lime, cut it in half and rub it on your forehead. The throbbing will go away.

17. Don't throw out all that leftover wine: Freeze into ice cubes for future use in casseroles and sauces.

18. If you have problem opening jars: Try using latex dishwashing gloves. They give a non-slip grip that makes opening jars easy.

19. Potatoes will take food stains off your fingers. Just slice and rub raw potato on the stains and rinse with water.

20. To get rid of itch from mosquito bite: try applying soap on the area for instant relief.

21. Ants are said to never cross a chalk line. So get your chalk out and draw a line on the floor or wherever ants tend to march and see for yourself.

22. Use air-freshener to clean mirrors: It does a good job and better still, leaves a lovely smell to the shine.

23. When you get a splinter, reach for the duct tape before resorting to tweezers or a needle. Simply put the duct tape over the splinter then pull it off. Duct tape removes most splinters painlessly and easily.

24. Look what you can do with Alka Seltzer: Clean a toilet. Drop in two Alka-Seltzer tablets, wait twenty minutes, brush, and flush. The citric acid and effervescent action clean vitreous china. Clean a vase. To remove a stain from the bottom of a glass vase or cruet, fill with water and drop in two Alka-Seltzer tablets. Polish jewelry. Drop two Alka-Seltzer tablets into a glass of water and immerse the jewelry for two minutes. Clean a thermos bottle. Fill the bottle with water, drop in four Alka-Seltzer tablets, and let soak for an hour (or longer, if necessary). Unclog a drain. Clear the sink drain by dropping three Alka-Seltzer tablets down the drain followed by a cup of Heinz White Vinegar Wait a few minutes, then run the hot water.

25. If your VCR has a year setting on it, which most do, you will not be able to use the programmed recording feature after 12/31/99. Don't throw it away. Instead set it for the year 1972 as the days are the same as the year 2000. The manufacturers won't tell you. They want you to buy a new Y2K VCR.

Real Life Stupidity

WITH A LITTLE HELP FROM OUR FRIENDS!

Police in California spent two hours attempting to subdue a gunman who had barricaded himself inside his home. After firing ten tear gas canisters, officers discovered that the man was standing beside them, shouting out to give himself up.

WHAT WAS PLAN B???

An Illinois man, pretending to have a gun, kidnapped a motorist and forced him to drive to two different automated teller machines. The kidnapper then proceeded to withdraw money from his own bank account.

SOME DAYS, IT JUST DOESN'T PAY!

Fire investigators on Maui have determined the cause of a blaze that destroyed a $127,000 home last month - a short in the homeowner's newly installed fire prevention alarm system. "This is even worse than last year," said the distraught homeowner, "when someone broke in and stole my new security system."

THE GETAWAY!

A man walked into a Topeka, Kansas convenience store and asked for all the money in the cash drawer. Apparently, the take was too small so he tied up the store clerk and worked the counter himself for three hours until police showed up and grabbed him.

DID I SAY THAT???

Police in Los Angeles had good luck with a robbery suspect who just couldn't control himself during a lineup. When detectives asked each man in the lineup to repeat the words, "Give me all your money or I'll shoot," the man shouted, "That's not what I said!"

OUCH, THAT SMARTS!!

A bank robber in Virginia Beach got a nasty surprise when a dye pack designed to mark stolen money exploded in his underpants. The robber apparently stuffed the loot down the front of his pants as he was running out the door. "He was seen hopping and jumping around with an explosion taking place inside his pants," said police spokesman Mike Carey. Police have the man's charred trousers in custody.

ARE WE ARE COMMUNICATING??

A man spoke frantically into the phone, "My wife is pregnant and her contractions are only two minutes apart!" "Is this her first child?" the doctor asked. "No, you idiot!" the man shouted, "This is her husband!"

NOT THE SHARPEST KNIFE IN THE DRAWER!!

In Modesto, CA, Steven Richard King was arrested for trying to hold up a Bank of America branch without a weapon. King used a thumb and a finger to simulate a gun but unfortunately he failed to keep his hand in his pocket.

<u>The Big Rocks In Your Life</u>

One day, an expert in the subject of time management was speaking to a group of business students. As this man stood in front of the group of high-powered over achievers, he said, "Okay, time for a quiz." He then pulled out a one gallon, wide-mouthed mason jar and set it on a table in front of him. He then produced about a dozen fist-sized rocks and carefully placed them, one at a time, into the jar. When the jar was filled to the top and no more rocks would fit inside, he asked, "Is this jar full?" Everyone in the class said, "Yes." Then, he said, "Really?" He reached under the table and pulled out a bucket of gravel. Then, he dumped some gravel in and shook the jar causing pieces of gravel to work themselves down into the spaces between the big rocks. Then, he asked the group once more, "Is the jar full?" By this time the class was onto him. "Probably not," one of them answered. "Good!" he replied. He reached under the table and brought out a bucket of sand. He started dumping the sand in and it went into all the spaces left between the rocks and the gravel. Once more, he asked the question, "Is this jar full?" "No!" the class shouted. Once again, he said, "Good!" Then, he grabbed a pitcher of water and began to pour it in until the jar was filled to the brim. Then, he looked up at the class and asked, "What is the point of this illustration?" One eager beaver raised his hand and said, "The point is, no matter how full your schedule is, if you try really hard, you can always fit some more things into it!" "No," the speaker replied, "that's not the point. The truth this illustration teaches us is the following: If you don't put the big rocks in first, you'll never get them in at all." What are the 'big rocks' in your life? Time with your loved ones? Your faith, your education, your finances? A cause? Teaching or mentoring others? Remember to put these BIG ROCKS in first or you'll never get them in at all.

Aimless Thoughts

Deep Thoughts

Life is sexually transmitted.

Kids in the back seat cause accidents; accidents in the back seat cause kids.

It's not the pace of life that concerns me, it's the sudden stop at the end.

The problem with the gene pool is that there is no lifeguard.

It's hard to make a comeback when you haven't been anywhere.

Living on Earth is expensive, but it does include a free trip around the sun.

The only time the world beats a path to your door is if you're in the bathroom.

If God wanted me to touch my toes, he would have put them on my knees.

Never knock on Death's door; ring the doorbell and run (he hates that).

Lead me not into temptation (I can find my own way).

When you're finally holding all the cards, why does everyone else decide to play chess?

If you're living on the edge, make sure you're wearing your seat belt.

The mind is like a parachute; it works much better when it's open.

Never take life too seriously. Nobody gets out alive anyway.

An unbreakable toy is useful for breaking other toys.

A closed mouth gathers no feet.

Good health is merely the slowest possible rate at which one can die.

It's not hard to meet expenses; they're everywhere.

Jury: Twelve people who determine which client has the better attorney.

The only difference between a rut and a grave is the depth.

Curious Thoughts
(ala Stephen Wright)

Last night I played a blank tape at full blast and the mime next door went nuts.

If a person with multiple personalities threatens suicide, is that considered a hostage situation?

Just think how much deeper the ocean would be if sponges didn't live there.

If a cow laughed, would milk come out her nose?

Whatever happened to preparations A through G?

If olive oil comes from olives then where does baby oil come from?

I went for a walk last night and my kids asked me how long I'd be gone. I said, "The whole time."

So, what IS the speed of dark?

How come you don't ever hear about gruntled employees? And, who has been dis-ing them anyhow?

After eating, do amphibians need to wait an hour before getting OUT of the water?

Why don't they just make mouse-flavored cat food?

If you're sending someone some Styrofoam, what do you pack it in?

I just got skylights put in my place and the people who live above me are furious.

Do they sterilize needles for lethal injections?

Do they have reserved parking for non-handicapped people at the Special Olympics?

Is it true that cannibals don't eat clowns because they taste funny?

When a man talks dirty to a woman, its sexual harassment. When a woman talks dirty to a man, it's $9.95 per minute.

If it's tourist season then why can't we shoot them?

Disney World: a people trap operated by a mouse.

Whose cruel idea was it for the word "lisp" to have an "s" in it?

Since light travels faster than sound, is that why some people appear bright until you hear them speak?

How come abbreviated is such a long word?

If it's zero degrees outside today and it's supposed to be twice as cold tomorrow, how cold is it going to be?

Why do you press harder on a remote-control when you know the battery is dead?

Since Americans throw rice at weddings. Do Asians throw hamburgers?

Why are they called buildings, when they're already finished? Shouldn't they be called builts?

Why are they called apartments, when they're all stuck together?

Why do banks charge you a "non-sufficient funds fee" on money they already know you don't have?

If the universe is everything, and scientists say that the universe is expanding, what is it expanding into?

If you got into a taxi and the driver started driving backward, would the taxi driver end up owing you money?

What would a chair look like if your knees bent the other way?

If a tree falls in the forest and no one is around to see it, do the other trees laugh at it?

Why is a carrot more orange than an orange?

When two airplanes almost collide why do they call it a near miss? It sounds like a near hit to me!

Do fish get cramps after eating?

Why are there 5 syllables in the word "monosyllabic?"

Why do they call it the Department of Interior when they are in charge of everything outdoors?

Why do scientists call it research when looking for something new?

If vegetarians eat vegetables, what do humanitarians eat?

When I delete a word on my computer, where does it go?

Why is it, when a door is open it's ajar, but when a jar is open, it's not a door?

Tell a man that there are 400 billion stars and he'll believe you. Tell him a bench has wet paint and he has to touch it.

How come Superman could stop bullets with his chest, but always ducked when someone threw a gun at him?

If "con" is the opposite of "pro," then what is the opposite of progress?

Why does lemon juice contain mostly artificial ingredients but dishwashing liquid contains real lemons?

Why buy a product that it takes 2000 flushes to get rid of?

Why do we wait until a pig is dead to "cure" it?

Why do we wash bath towels? Aren't we clean when we use them?

Why do we put suits in a garment bag and put garments in a suitcase?

Why doesn't glue stick to the inside of the bottle?

Do Roman paramedics refer to IV's as "4's?"

What do little birdies see when they get knocked unconscious?

Why doesn't Tarzan have a beard?

If man evolved from monkeys and apes, why do we still have monkeys and apes?

Should you trust a stockbroker who's married to a travel agent?

Is boneless chicken considered to be an invertebrate?

Do married people truly live longer than single people or does it just SEEM longer?

I went to a bookstore and asked the saleswoman, "Where's the self-help section?"
She said if she told me, it would defeat the purpose.

If all those psychics know the future, why aren't they buying up the winning lottery tickets?

Isn't the best way to save face to keep the lower part shut?

War doesn't determine who's right, just who's left.

One tequila, two tequila, three tequila, floor.

Santa is very jolly because he knows where all the bad girls live.

Should crematoriums give discounts for burn victims?

If a mute swears, does his mother wash his hands with soap?

If a man stands in the middle of the forest speaking and there isn't a woman around to hear him, is he still wrong?

<u>Some Cute Thoughts</u>

Everyone has a photographic memory. Some just don't have film in the camera.

Save the whales. Collect the whole set.

A day without sunshine is like, night.

On the other hand, you have five different fingers.

I just got lost in thought. It was unfamiliar territory.

When the chips are down, the buffalo is empty.

Those who live by the sword get shot by those who don't.

I feel like I'm diagonally parked in a parallel universe.

You have the right to remain silent. Anything you say will be misquoted then used against you.

Honk if you love peace and quiet.

Pardon my driving; I'm reloading.

Despite the cost of living, have you noticed how it remains so popular?

Nothing is fool-proof to a sufficiently talented fool.

Atheism is a non-prophet organization.

He who laughs last, thinks slowest.

It is well to remember that the entire universe, with one trifling exception, is composed of others.

Depression is merely anger without enthusiasm.

Eagles may soar, but weasels don't get sucked into jet engines.

The early bird gets the worm, but the second mouse gets the cheese.

I'm not cheap, but I AM on special this week.

I almost had a psychic girlfriend but she left me before we met.

I drive way too fast to worry about cholesterol.

I intend to live forever; so far, so good.

I love defenseless animals, especially in a good gravy.

If Barbie is so popular, why do you have to buy her friends?

Mind Like A Steel Trap: Rusty And Illegal In 37 States.

Quantum Mechanics: The dreams stuff is made of.

Support bacteria; They're the only culture some people have.

The only substitute for good manners is fast reflexes.

When everything's coming your way, you're in the wrong lane, going the wrong way.

If at first you don't succeed, destroy all evidence that you tried.

A conclusion is the place where you got tired of thinking.

Experience is something you don't get until just after you need it.

For every action, there is an equal and opposite criticism.

He who hesitates is probably right.

Never do card tricks for the group you play poker with.

No one is listening until you make a mistake.

Success always occurs in private, and failure in full view.

The colder the X-ray table, the more of your body that is required on it.

The hardness of the butter is directly proportional to the softness of the bread.

The severity of the itch is inversely proportional to the ability to reach it.

To steal ideas from one person is plagiarism; to steal from many is research.

To succeed in politics, it is often necessary to rise above your principles.

Two wrongs don't make a right, but it usually makes a good start to a funny story.

You never really learn to swear until you learn to drive.

Monday is an awful way to spend 1/7th of your life.

The sooner you fall behind, the more time you'll have to catch up.

A clear conscience is usually the sign of a bad memory.

If you must choose between two evils, pick the one you've never tried before.

Change is inevitable....except from vending machines.

A fool and his money are soon partying.

Plan to be spontaneous tomorrow.

<u>People Are The Strangest Animals</u>

SMART MAN + SMART WOMAN = ROMANCE

SMART MAN + DUMB WOMAN = PREGNANCY

DUMB MAN + SMART WOMAN = AFFAIR

DUMB MAN + DUMB WOMAN = MARRIAGE

SMART BOSS + SMART EMPLOYEE = PROFITS

SMART BOSS + DUMB EMPLOYEE = PRODUCTION

DUMB BOSS + SMART EMPLOYEE = PROMOTION

DUMB BOSS + DUMB EMPLOYEE = OVERTIME

A MAN WILL PAY $2.00 FOR A $1.00 ITEM HE NEEDS.
WOMAN WILL PAY $1.00 FOR A $2.00 ITEM THAT SHE DOES NOT NEED.

A WOMAN WORRIES ABOUT THE FUTURE UNTIL SHE GETS A
HUSBAND.
A MAN NEVER WORRIES ABOUT THE FUTURE UNTIL HE GETS A WIFE.

A SUCCESSFUL MAN IS ONE WHO MAKES MORE MONEY THAN HIS
    WIFE CAN SPEND.
A SUCCESSFUL WOMAN IS ONE WHO CAN FIND SUCH A MAN.

TO BE HAPPY WITH A MAN, YOU MUST LOVE HIM A LITTLE AND
    UNDERSTAND HIM A LOT.
TO BE HAPPY WITH A WOMAN YOU MUST LOVE HER A LOT AND NOT
    TRY TO UNDERSTAND HER AT ALL.

MEN WAKE UP AS GOOD-LOOKING AS THEY WENT TO BED.
WOMEN SOMEHOW DETERIORATE OVERNIGHT.

A WOMAN MARRIES A MAN EXPECTING HE WILL CHANGE, BUT HE
DOESN'T.
A MAN MARRIES A WOMAN EXPECTING SHE WON'T CHANGE, BUT
SHE DOES.

MARRIED MEN LIVE LONGER THAN SINGLE MEN, BUT MARRIED MEN
    ARE MORE WILLING TO DIE.

ANY MARRIED MAN SHOULD FORGET HIS MISTAKES. THERE'S NO USE IN TWO PEOPLE REMEMBERING THE SAME THING.

A WOMAN HAS THE LAST WORD IN ANY ARGUMENT. ANYTHING A MAN SAYS AFTER THAT IS THE BEGINNING OF A NEW ARGUMENT.

Humorous Thoughts

I ALWAYS GIVE 100% AT WORK:
12% Monday
23% Tuesday
40% Wednesday
20% Thursday
5% Friday

Failure is not an option! It comes bundled with the software.

I want to die while asleep like my Grandfather, not screaming in terror like the passengers in his car.

I can't dial 911. There's no 11 on my phone.

KENTUCKY: Five Million People, Fifteen Last Names.

JESUS LOVES YOU. It's everybody else that thinks you're an ass.

I married Miss Right. I just didn't know her first name was, "Always."

What is a free gift?   Aren't all gifts free?

Can you yell "MOVIE!" in a crowded fire station?

It's hard to make a comeback when you haven't been anywhere.

If ignorance is bliss, why aren't more people happy?

To vacillate or not to vacillate, that is the question....or is it?

Sometimes I wake up grumpy. Other times I let her sleep.

I didn't fight my way to the top of the food chain to be a vegetarian.

Don't get married; just pick a woman you hate and buy her a house.

Be nice to your kids. They will be choosing your nursing home.

I still miss my ex. But, my aim is getting better!

I haven't spoken to my wife in 2 months. She gets mad if I interrupt her.

Very funny, Scotty. Now beam down my clothes.

A closed mouth gathers no foot.

If women can have PMS, then men can have ESPN.

First draw the curve, then plot the data.

When blondes have more fun, do they know it?

Where there's smoke, there's dinner.

Losing a wife can be hard. In my case it was almost impossible.

Always try to be modest. And, be proud of it!

If you think nobody cares about you, try missing a couple of payments.

How many of you believe in telekinesis? Raise my hands....

Get a new car for your spouse; it'll be a great trade!

Drugs may lead to nowhere, but at least it's the scenic route.

I'd kill for a Nobel Peace Prize.

Everybody repeat after me....."We are all individuals."

Death to all fanatics!

Love may be blind, but marriage is a real eye-opener.

Hell hath no fury like the lawyer of a woman scorned.

Bills travel through the mail at twice the speed of checks.

Hard work pays off in the future. Laziness pays off now.

Borrow money from pessimists-they don't expect it back.

Half the people you know are below average.

99 percent of lawyers give the rest a bad name.

42.7 percent of all statistics are made up on the spot.

A conscience is what hurts when all your other parts feel so good.

If at first you don't succeed, then skydiving definitely isn't for you.

Nonconformists unite.

Dyslexics untie.

Questions That Need To Be Answered

1. Can fat people go skinny dipping?

2. Do kamikaze pilots wear helmets?

3. Can you be a closet claustrophobic?

4. If a turtle does not have a shell, is he homeless or naked?

5. Is it possible to be totally partial?

6. What's another word for thesaurus?

7. If a book about failures doesn't sell is it a success?

8. If you are cross-eyed and have dyslexia, can you read correctly?

9. If a stealth bomber crashes in a forest is there a sound?

10. If a parsley farmer is sued, do they garnish his wages?

11. When it rains, why don't sheep shrink?

12. Should vegetarians avoid eating animal crackers?

13. Do cemetery workers prefer the graveyard shift?

14. What do you do when an endangered animal eats endangered plants?

15. Do hungry cows have ravenous appetites?

16. Why is bra singular and panties plural?

17. Why do they lock gas station bathrooms? Are they afraid someone will clean them?

18. Would a fly without wings be a walk?

19. Is there another word for synonym?

20. Isn't it a bit unnerving that doctors call what they do "practice?"

21. When sign makers go on strike, is anything printed on their signs?

22. When you open a bag of cotton balls, is the top one meant to be thrown away?

23. Where do forest rangers go to "get away from it all?"

24. Why do they put Braille on the drive-through bank machines?

25. How do they get the deer to cross at that yellow road sign?

26. What was the best thing before sliced bread?

Old And New Concerns For People Of The Baby Boom Generation

Then: Long hair.
Now: Longing for hair.

Then: Keg
Now: EKG.

Then: Acid rock
Now: Acid reflux.

Then: Moving to California because it's cool.
Now: Moving to California because it's hot.

Then: You're growing pot.
Now: Your growing pot.

Then: Watching John Glenn's historic flight with your parents.
Now: Watching John Glenn's historic flight with your kids.

Then: Trying to look like Marlon Brando or Elizabeth Taylor.
Now: Trying not to look like Marlon Brando or Elizabeth Taylor.

Then: Seeds and stems.
Now: Roughage.

Then: Popping pills, smoking joints.
Now: Popping joints.

Then: Our president's struggle with Fidel.
Now: Our president's struggle with fidelity.

Then: Paar.
Now: AARP.

Then: Being caught with Hustler magazine.
Now: Being caught by Hustler magazine.

Then: Killer weed.
Now: Weed killer.

Then: Hoping for a BMW.
Now: Hoping for a BM.

Then: The Grateful Dead.
Now: Dr. Kevorkian.

Then: Getting out to a new, hip joint.
Now: Getting a new hip joint.

Rodney Dangerfield's Best One Liners

A girl phoned me the other day and said, "Come on over, there's nobody home." I went over. Nobody was home.

During sex, my girlfriend always wants to talk to me. Just the other night she called me from a hotel.

I was so ugly as a child, when I played in the sandbox the cat kept covering me up.

I could tell that my parents hated me. My bath toys were a toaster and a radio.

My father carries around the picture of the kid who came with his wallet.

When I was born, the doctor came out to the waiting room and said to my father, "I'm very sorry. We did everything we could but he pulled through."

My mother had morning sickness after I was born.

I remember the time I was kidnapped and they sent a piece of my finger to my father. He said he wanted more proof.

Once when I was lost..... I saw a policeman and asked him to help me find my parents. I said to him, "Do you think we'll ever find them?" He said, "I don't know kid, there are so many places they can hide."

On Halloween, the parents send their kids out looking like me. Last year, one kid tried to rip my face off! Now it's different, when I answer the door the kids hand me candy.

My wife made me join a bridge club. I jump off next Tuesday.

I worked in a pet shop and people kept asking how big I'd get.

I went to see my doctor. Doctor, every morning when I get up and look in the mirror, I feel like throwing up. What's wrong with me? He said, "I don't know, but your eyesight is perfect."

My psychiatrist told me I'm going crazy. I told him, "If you don't mind, I'd like a second opinion." He said, "Alright, you're ugly too!"

When I was born the doctor took one look at my face, turned me over and said, "Look, twins!"

I remember when I swallowed a bottle of sleeping pills. My doctor told me to have a few drinks and get some rest.

If you're an Andy Rooney fan... You'll like these thoughts ....

Ads in Bills:

    Have you ever noticed that they put advertisements in with your bills now? Like bills aren't distasteful enough, they have to stuff junk mail in with them. I get back at them. I put garbage in with my check when I mail it in. Coffee grinds, banana peels...I write, "Could you throw this away for me? Thank you."

Fabric Softener:

    My wife uses fabric softener. I never knew what that stuff was for. Then, I noticed women were coming up to me (sniff) 'Married' (walk off). That's how they mark their territory. You can take off that ring, but it's hard to get that April fresh scent out of your clothes.

Cripes:

    My wife's from the Midwest. Very nice people there. Very wholesome. They use words like 'Cripes.' For Cripe's sake. Who would that be, Jesus Cripes? The son of 'Gosh?' of the church of 'Holy Moly'. I'm not making fun of it. You think I wanna burn in 'Heck'?

Morning Differences:

    Men and women are different in the morning. The men wake up aroused in the morning. We can't help it. We just wake up and we want you. And, the women are thinking, 'how can he want me the way I look in the morning?' It's because we can't see you. We have no blood anywhere near our optic nerve.

Pregnancy:

    It's weird when pregnant women feel the baby kicking. They say, 'Oh my god. He's kicking. Do you wanna feel it?' I always feel awkward reaching over there. Come on! It's weird to ask someone to feel your stomach. I don't do that when I have gas. "Oh my god...give me your hand...It won't be long now..."

Grandma:

    My grandmother has a bumper sticker on her car that says, 'Sexy Senior Citizen'. You don't want to think of your grandmother that way, do you? Out entering wet shawl contests. Makes you wonder where she got that dollar she gave you for your birthday.

Prisons:

    Did you know that it costs forty thousand dollars a year to house each prisoner? Jeez, for forty thousand bucks a piece I'll take a few prisoners into my house. I live in Los Angeles. I already have bars on the windows. I don't think we should give free room and board to criminals. I think they should have to run twelve hours a day on a treadmill and generate electricity. And, if they don't want to run, they can rest in the chair that's hooked up to the generator.

Award Shows:

     Can you believe how many award shows they have now? They have awards for commercials. The Clio Awards. A whole show full of commercials. I taped it and then I fast-forwarded through the whole thing.

Phone-in Polls:

     You know those shows where people call in and vote on different issues? Did you ever notice there's always like 18% "I don't know." It costs 90 cents to call up and vote... They're voting "I don't know." "Honey, I feel very strongly about this. Give me the phone. (Into phone) I DON'T KNOW! (hangs up, looking proud) Sometimes you have to stand up for what you believe you're not sure about." This guy probably calls up phone sex girls for $9.95 to say, "I'm not in the mood."

Answering Machine:

     Did you ever hear one of those corny, positive messages on someone's answering machine? "Hi, it's a great day and I'm out enjoying it right now. I hope you are too. The thought for the day is 'Share the love'." Beep. "Uh, yeah...this is the VD clinic calling...Speaking of being positive, your test is back. Stop sharing the love."

The Drunk Poem

* *   Starkle, starkle, little twink,*
  *   *   *
 *   Who the hell are you I think. * *
     *   *   *
* *   I'm not under what you call *
     *   *   *
 *   The alcofluence of incohol. * *
    *   *   *
* * I'm just a little slort of sheep, *
   *   *   *
  * I'm not drunk like thinkle peep. * *
 *   *   *
* *   I don't know who is me yet, *
   *   *   *
 *   But the drunker I stand here the longer I get. * *
   *   *   *   *   *
* *   So just give me one more fink to drill my cup, *
   *   *   *   *
 *   'Cause I got all day sober to Sunday up. * *
   *   *   *   *   *   *

Spam Haikus

1.
Blue can of steel
What promise do you hold?
Salt flesh so ripe

2.
Can of metal, slick
Soft center, so cool, moistening
I yearn for your salt

3.
Twist, pull the sharp lid
Jerks and cuts me deeply but
Spam, aah, my poultice

4.
Silent, former pig
One communal awareness
Myriad pink bricks

5.
Clad in metal, proud
No mere salt-curing for you
You are not bacon

6
And who dares mock Spam?
You? you? you are not worthy
Of one rich pink fleck

7.
Like some spongy rock
A granite, my piece of Spam
In sunlight on my plate

8.
Little slab of meat
In a wash of clear jelly
Now I heat the pan

9.
Oh tin of pink meat
I ponder what you may be:
Snout or ear or feet?

10.
In the cool morning
I fry up a slab of Spam
A dog barks next door

11.
Pink tender morsel
Glistening with salty gel
What the hell is it?

12.
Ears, snouts and innards
A homogeneous mass
Pass another slice

13.
Old man seeks doctor
"I eat Spam daily," he says.
Angioplasty

14.
Highly unnatural
The tortured shape of this "food"
A small pink coffin

15.
Pink beefy temptress
I can no longer remain
Vegetarian

Why We're All So Damn Tired

For a couple years, I've been blaming it on iron-poor blood, lack of vitamins, dieting and a dozen other maladies. But, now I found out the real reason. I'm tired because I'm overworked!!!!! The population of this country is 237 million. 104 million are retired. That leaves 133 million to do the work. There are 85 million in school, which leave 48 million to do the work. Of this, there are 29 million employed by the federal government. This leaves 19 million to do the work. Four million are in the Armed Forces, which leaves 15 million to do the work. Take from the total the 14,800,000 people who work for State and City Government and that leaves 200,000 to do the work. There are 188,000 in hospitals, so that leaves 12,000 to do the work. Now, there are 11,998 people in prisons. That leaves just two people to do the work. You and me. And, you're sitting there screwing around reading this nonsense.

Rest Room Signs

Friends don't let friends take home ugly women.

If you can piss this high, join the fire department. (Men's restroom wall, 6 feet high.)

Beauty is only a light switch away.

I've decided that to raise my grades I must lower my standards.

If life is a waste of time, and time is a waste of life, then let's all get wasted together and have the time of our lives.

Remember, it's not, "How high are you?" It's "Hi, how are you?"

God made pot. Man made beer. Who do you trust?

Fighting for peace is like screwing for virginity.

No matter how good she looks, if she's single it means some other guy is sick and tired of putting up with her crap.

To do is to be. -Descartes
To be is to do. -Voltaire
Do be do be do. -Frank Sinatra

At the feast of ego, everyone leaves hungry.

Make love, not war.-Hell, do both, get married!

God is dead. -Nietzsche
Nietzsche is dead. -God

If voting could really change things, it would be illegal.

A Woman's Rule of Thumb: If it has tires or testicles, you're going to have trouble with it.

JESUS SAVES! But, wouldn't it be better if he had invested?

Watch out for Gay Limbo Dancers (On the bottom edge of the toilet stall wall.)

Express Lane: Five beers or less.

You're too good for him. (Sign over mirror in Women's restroom.)

No wonder you always go home alone. (Sign over mirror in Men's restroom.)

Alcohol Helps

A herd of buffalo can only move as fast as the slowest buffalo, and when the herd is hunted, it is the slowest and weakest ones at the back that are killed first. This natural selection is good for the herd as a whole, because the general speed and health of the whole group keeps improving by the regular attrition of the weakest members. In much the same way, the human brain can only operate as fast as the slowest brain cells. Excessive intake of alcohol, we all know, kills brain cells, but naturally it attacks the slowest and weakest brain cells first. In this way, regular consumption of alcohol eliminates the weaker brain cells, making the brain a faster and more efficient machine. That's why you always feel smarter after a few drinks.

Bumper Stickers You May Relate To

If You Can Read This, I Can Slam On My Brakes And Sue You.

1,000,000 Sperm And YOU Were The Fastest???

Forget Visualizing World Peace..........Visualize Turning Off Your Turn Signal!

HANG UP AND DRIVE!

Where There's A Will..........I Want To Be In It!

Ever Stop To Think, And Forget To Start Again?

I Have The Body Of A God..........Buddha

This Would Be Really Funny If It Weren't Happening To Me.

If We Quit Voting Will They All Go Away?

This Bumper Sticker Exploits Illiterates.

Eat Right, Exercise, Die Anyway.

Honk If Anything Falls Off.

He Who Hesitates Is Not Only Lost, But Miles From The Next Exit.

I Haven't Lost My Mind..........It's Backed Up On Disk Somewhere.

Interesting Thoughts

1. I think animal testing is a terrible idea; they get all nervous and give the wrong answers.
--A Bit of Fry and Laurie

2. A Freudian slip is when you say one thing but mean your mother.

3. The hypothalamus is one of the most important parts of the brain, involved in many kinds of motivation, among other functions. The hypothalamus controls the "Four F's": 1. fighting; 2. fleeing; 3. feeding; and 4. mating.
-- Psychology professor in neuropsychology intro course

4. Slogan of the classic rock radio station in Chicago: "Of all the radio stations in Chicago...we're one of them."

5. Applying computer technology is simply finding the right wrench to pound in the correct screw.

6. Karate is a form of martial arts in which people who have had years and years of training can, using only their hands and feet, make some of the worst movies in the history of the world.
-- Dave Barry

7. I am not a vegetarian because I love animals; I am a vegetarian because I hate plants.
-- A. Whitney Brown

8. A great many people think they are thinking when they are merely rearranging their prejudices.
--William James

9. If a woman has to choose between catching a fly ball and saving an infant's life, she will choose to save the infant's life without even considering if there are men on base.
-- Dave Barry

10. When cryptography is outlawed, bayl bhgynjf jvyy unir cevinpl.

11. Lazlo's Chinese Relativity Axiom: No matter how great your triumphs or how tragic your defeats ---approximately one billion Chinese couldn't care less.

12. Some mornings, it's just not worth chewing through the leather straps.
-- Emo Phillips

13. Writing about music is like dancing about architecture.

14. When I told the people of Northern Ireland that I was an atheist, a woman in the audience stood up and said, "Yes, but is it the God of the Catholics or the God of the Protestants in whom you don't believe?"
-- Quentin Crisp

15. Boundary, n. In political geography, an imaginary line between two nations, separating the imaginary rights of one from the imaginary rights of another.
-- Ambrose Bierce, The Devil's Dictionary

16. May the forces of evil become confused on the way to your house.
-- George Carlin

17. Life may have no meaning. Or even worse, it may have a meaning of which I disapprove.
-- Ashleigh Brilliant

18. My opinions may have changed, but not the fact that I am right.
-- Ashleigh Brilliant

19. Once at a social gathering, Gladstone said to Disraeli, "I predict, Sir, that you will die either by hanging or of some vile disease." Disraeli replied, "That all depends, sir, upon whether I embrace your principles or your mistress."

20. For three days after death, hair and fingernails continue to grow but phone calls taper off.
-- Johnny Carson

21. My initial response was to sue her for defamation of character, but then I realized that I had no character.
-- Charles Barkley, on hearing Tonya Harding proclaim herself "the Charles Barkley of figure skating"

22. The most important thing in the programming language is the name. A language will not succeed without a good name. I have recently invented a very good name and now I am looking for a suitable language.
-- D. E. Knuth, 1967

23. Suppose you were an idiot. And, suppose you were a member of Congress. But, I repeat myself.
-- Mark Twain

24. On one occasion a student burst into his office. "Professor Stigler, I don't believe I deserve this F you've given me." To which Stigler replied, "I agree, but unfortunately it is the lowest grade the University will allow me to award."

25. The overwhelming majority of people have more than the average (mean) number of legs.
-- E. Grebenik

26. G: "If we do happen to step on a mine, Sir, what do we do?"
    EB: "Normal procedure, Lieutenant, is to jump 200 feet in the air and scatter oneself over a wide area."
-- Somewhere in No Man's Land, BA4

27. I hate to advocate drugs, alcohol, violence, or insanity to anyone, but they've always worked for me.
-- Hunter S. Thompson

28. I am amazed at radio DJs today. I am firmly convinced that AM stands for Absolute Moron. I will not begin to tell you what FM stands for.
-- Jasper Carrott

Things That Bother Me

The Pillsbury doughboy is way too happy considering he has no genitals.

When something is "new and improved," which is it? If it's new, then there has never been anything before it. If it's an improvement, then there must have been something before it. And, if it is really an improvement, just how crappy was the original product.

People who are willing to get off their ass to search the room for the TV remote because they refuse to walk to the TV and change the channel manually.

When people say "It's always in the last place you look." Of course it is. Why would you keep looking after you've found it? Do people do this? Who and where are they?

The radio ad "Hi, I'm Jeff Healey from the Jeff Healey Band. Don't drink and drive. I don't." Well, I hope you don't drive sober either Mr. Healey. You're blind for god's sake!

People who ask, "Can I ask you a question?" Didn't really give me a choice, did ya there buddy?

People who point at their wrist while asking for the time. I know where my watch is buddy, where the hell is yours? Do I point at my crotch when I ask where the bathroom is?

Classic Drinking Quotes

Time is never wasted when you're wasted all the time.
--Catherine Zandonella

Abstainer: a weak person who yields to the temptation of denying himself a pleasure.
--Ambrose Bierce

I never drink anything stronger than gin before breakfast.
A woman drove me to drink and I didn't even have the decency to thank her.
What contemptible scoundrel has stolen the cork to my lunch?
--W.C. Fields

"The best way to get most husbands to do something is to suggest that perhaps they're too old to do it."
--Ann Bancroft

Beauty lies in the hands of the beer holder.

Sir, if you were my husband, I would poison your drink.
--Lady Astor to Winston Churchill
Madam, if you were my wife, I would drink it.
--His reply

If God had intended us to drink beer, He would have given us stomachs.
--David Daye

My problem with most athletic challenges is training. I'm lazy and find that workouts cut into my drinking time.
--A Wolverine is Eating My Leg

Work is the curse of the drinking classes.
--Oscar Wilde

When I read about the evils of drinking, I gave up reading.
--Henny Youngman

Life is a waste of time, time is a waste of life, so get wasted all of the time and have the time of your life.

I'd rather have a bottle in front of me, than a frontal lobotomy.
--Tom Waits

Put it back in the horse
-H. Allen Smith, an American humorist in the '30s-'50s, after his first American beer at a bar.

You don't like jail?
Naw, they got the wrong kind of bars in there.
-Charles Bukowski

If you ever reach total enlightenment while drinking beer, I bet it makes beer shoot out your nose.
--Deep Thought, Jack Handy

Life is too short to drink cheap beer.

Beer - it's not just for breakfast anymore

Beer: Nature's laxative.

One more drink and I'd be under the host.
--Dorothy Parker

When I heated my home with oil, I used an average of 800 gallons a year. I have found that I can keep comfortably warm for an entire winter with slightly over half that quantity of beer.
--Postpetroleum Guzzler, Dave Barry

Without question, the greatest invention in the history of mankind is beer. Oh, I grant you that the wheel was also a fine invention, but the wheel does not go nearly as well with pizza.
--Dave Barry's Bad Habits, Dave Barry

Not all chemicals are bad. Without chemicals such as hydrogen and oxygen, for example, there would be no way to make water, a vital ingredient in beer.
--Dave Barry

The problem with the world is that everyone is a few drinks behind.
--Humphrey Bogart

Draft beer, not people!

Adhere to Schweinheitsgebot. Don't put anything in your beer that a pig wouldn't eat.
--David Geary

Why is American beer served cold? So, you can tell it from urine.
--David Moulton

A drink a day keeps the shrink away.
--Edward Abbey

24 hours in a day, 24 beers in a case. Coincidence?

T-Shirt Slogans

"Filthy, Stinking Rich -- Well, Two Out of Three Ain't Bad"

"Real Men Don't Waste Their Hormones Growing Hair"

"Upon the Advice of My Attorney, My Shirt Bears No Message at This Time"

"Frankly, Scallop, I Don't Give a Clam" -- seen on Cape Cod

"Happiness Is Seeing Your Mother-in-law on a Milk Carton"

"That's It! I'm Calling Grandma!" - (seen on an 8 year old)

"Wrinkled Was Not One of the Things I Wanted to Be When I Grew Up"

"Procrastinate Now"

"Rehab Is for Quitters"

"My Husband and I Married for Better or Worse - He Couldn't Do Better and I Couldn't Do Worse"

"My Dog Can Lick Anyone"

"I Have a Degree in Liberal Arts -- Do You Want Fries With That?"

"Party -- My Crib - Two A.M." (On a baby-size shirt)

"Finally 21, and Legally Able to Do Everything I've Been Doing Since 15"

"If a woman's place is in the home WHY AM I ALWAYS IN THIS CAR!"

"ALL MEN ARE IDIOTS, AND I MARRIED THEIR KING"

"West Virginia: One Million People, Fifteen Last Names"

"FAILURE IS NOT AN OPTION. It comes bundled with the software."

"I'M OUT OF ESTROGEN AND I'VE GOT A GUN"

"A hangover is the wrath of grapes"

"A journey of a thousand miles begins with a cash advance"

"STUPIDITY IS NOT A HANDICAP. Park elsewhere!"

"DISCOURAGE INBREEDING - Ban Country Music"

"Where there's a will I want to be in it"

"MOOSEHEAD: A great beer and a new experience for a moose"

"They call it "PMS" because "Mad Cow Disease" was already taken"

"How long is this Beta guy going to keep testing our stuff?"

"He who dies with the most toys is nonetheless dead"

"Time's fun when you're having flies.......Kermit the Frog"

"POLICE STATION TOILET STOLEN ....Cops have nothing to go on."

"If the shoe fits, buy it.----Imelda Marcos"

"HECK IS WHERE PEOPLE GO WHO DON'T BELIEVE IN GOSH"

"A PICTURE IS WORTH A THOUSAND WORDS--But it uses up a thousand times the memory."

"The Meek shall inherit the earth....after we're through with it."

"Time flies like an arrow. Fruit flies like a banana."

"HAM AND EGGS - A day's work for a chicken; A lifetime commitment for a pig."

"HARD WORK WILL PAY OFF LATER. LAZINESS PAYS OFF NOW!"

"WELCOME TO KENTUCKY - Set your watch back 20 years."

"The trouble with life is there's no background music."

"IF THERE IS NO GOD, WHO POPS UP THE NEXT KLEENEX?"

"Suicidal Twin Kills Sister By Mistake!"

"The original point and click interface was a Smith & Wesson."

"Two rights do not make a wrong. They make an airplane."

"MY WILD OATS HAVE TURNED TO SHREDDED WHEAT"

"Automobile: A mechanical device that runs up hills and down people.

"Computer programmers don't byte, they nibble a bit."

"Computer programmers know how to use their hardware."

"MOP AND GLOW: Floor wax used by Three Mile Island cleanup team.

"NyQuil - The stuffy, sneezy, why-the-hell-is-the-room-spinning medicine."

I saw a guy in Florida last year wearing a shirt with a Harley Davidson logo on the front. The back said, "IF YOU CAN READ THIS, THE BITCH FELL OFF AGAIN!"

"My husband and I divorced over religious differences - He thought he was God and I didn't!"

J.D. Heskin

So Many Lists

Relatives Of Vincent Van Gogh

His obnoxious brother - Please Gogh

The brother who ate lots of prunes - Gotta Gogh

The brother who worked at the convenience store - Stopn Gogh

The grandfather from Yugoslavia - U Gogh

The brother who bleached his clothes white - Hue Gogh

His dizzy aunt - Verti Gogh

The cousin in Illinois   - Chica Gogh

His magician uncle - Warediddy Gogh

His Mexican uncle - Amee Gogh

The Mexican cousin's half brother - Grin Gogh

The nephew who drove a stagecoach - Wellsfar Gogh

The constipated uncle - Cant Gogh

The ballroom dancing aunt - Tan Gogh

The bird lover uncle - Flamin Gogh

His nephew psychoanalyst - E Gogh

The fruit loving cousin - Man Gogh

An aunt who taught positive thinking - Wayto Gogh

The little nephew - Poe Gogh

A sister who loved to Disco - Go Gogh

And, his niece that travels in a van - Winniebay Gogh

I think there was also a distant relative named Far Gogh.

A Cynic's Rules For Work

1. Never give me work in the morning. Always wait until 4:00 and then bring it to me. The challenge of a deadline is refreshing.

2. If it's really a rush job, run in and interrupt me every 10 minutes to inquire how it's going. That helps. Or even better, hover behind me, advising me at every keystroke.

3. Always leave without telling anyone where you're going. It gives me a chance to be creative when someone asks where you are.

4. If my arms are full of papers, boxes, books, or supplies, don't open the door for me. I need to learn how to function as a paraplegic and opening doors with no arms is good training in case I should ever be injured and lose all use of my limbs.

5. If you give me more than one job to do, don't tell me which is the priority. I am psychic.

6. Do your best to keep me late. I adore this office and really have nowhere to go or anything to do. I have no life beyond work.

7. If a job I do pleases you, keep it a secret. If that gets out, it could mean a promotion.

8. If you don't like my work, tell everyone. I like my name to be popular in conversations. I was born to be whipped.

9. If you have special instructions for a job, don't write them down. In fact, save them until the job is almost done. No use confusing me with useful information.

10. Never introduce me to the people you're with. I have no right to know anything. In the corporate food chain, I am plankton. When you refer to them later, my shrewd deductions will identify them.

11. Be nice to me only when the job I'm doing for you could really change your life and send you straight to manager's hell.

12. Tell me all your little problems. No one else has any and it's nice to know someone is less fortunate. I especially like the story about having to pay so much taxes on the bonus check you received for being such a good manager.

13. Wait until my yearly review and THEN tell me what my goals SHOULD have been. Give me a mediocre performance rating with a cost of living increase. I'm not here for the money anyway.

The Poopie List

Ghost Poopie: The kind where you feel it come out, but there is no poopie in the toilet.

Clean Poopie: The kind where you poopie it out, see it in the toilet, but there is nothing on the toilet paper.

Wet Poopie: The kind where you wipe your butt 50 times and still feels unwipped, so you have to put some toilet paper between your butt and your underwear, so you won't ruin them with a stain.

Second Wave Poopie: This happens when you're done poopieing and you've pulled your pants up to your knees and you realize that you have to poopie some more.

Pop-A-Vein-In-Your-Forehead-Poopie: The kind were you strain so much to get it out, you practically have a stroke.

Lincoln Log Poopie: The kind of poopie that is so huge, your afraid to flush without first breaking it into little pieces with the toilet brush.

Gassy Poopie: It's so noisy, everyone within earshot is giggling.

Corn Poopie: Self explanatory.

Gee-I-Wish-I-Could-Poopie Poopie: The kind where you want to poopie, but all you do is sit on the toilet and fart a few times.

Spinal Tap Poopie: That's where it hurts so bad coming out, you swear its leaving sideways.

Wet Cheeks Poopie: (The power dump) The kind that comes out of your butt so fast, your cheeks get splashed with water.

Liquid Poopie: The kind where yellowish-brown liquid shoots out of your butt and splashes all over the toilet bowl.

Mexican Poopie: It smells so bad your nose burns.

Upper Class Poopie: The kind of poopie that doesn't smell.

The Surprise Poopie: You are not even at the toilet because you are sure your about to fart, but OOPS!- a poopie!

The Dangling Poopie: This poopie refuses to drop into the toilet even though you know you are done poopieing. You just pray that a shake or two will cut it loose.

<u>You Might Be A Minnesotan If…</u>

….You measure distance in minutes.

….Weather is 80% of your conversation.

….Down south to you means Iowa.

….Snow tires can come standard on your car.

….You have no concept of public transportation.

….75% of your graduating high school class went to the University of Minnesota.

….People from other states love to hear you say words with "O"s in them.

….You know what "Dinkytown" is.

…."Perkins" and "McDonald's" were the only hangout option in high school.

….You have no problem spelling "Minneapolis."

….You can list all the "Dales."

….You hate the movie "Fargo" but know that your entire family has the accent.

….You get mad at people who think Fargo is in Minnesota.

….Your school classes have been canceled because of cold.

…..You know what Mille Lacs is and how to spell it.

….You know when you say "The Cities" people know which cities you're referring to.

….You know what the numbers 6-94, 4-94, I-94, 3-94 mean.

….You have boiled fish in lye for Christmas or personally know someone who has.

….Nothing gets you madder than seeing a Green Bay Sticker on a Minnesota Car!!!

….You know what "uff-da" means and how to use it properly.

….You can spot the 3 second cameo appearance by "The Artist formerly known as Prince" in "Fargo."

….You're a loyal Target shopper.

….You know that the Gay 90s is now "Bi."

….You've licked frozen metal.

….The only reason you go to Wisconsin is to get fireworks.

….You own an ice house, a snowmobile, and a 4 wheel drive vehicle.

….You wear shorts when it's 50 degrees outside in March, but bundle up and complain in August when it goes below 60.

….You know people who have more fishing poles than teeth.

….You remember WLOL.

….It feels like the Mississippi is everywhere you go.

….When you talk about an "opener" you are not talking about cans.

….You have gone Trick-or-Treating in 3 feet of snow.

….You know that when it comes to AM, there is only 'CCO, besides, what else do you need?

….You know what the word SPAM stands for.

….You carry jumper cables in your car.

….You drink "POP."

….In a conversation someone said, "yah sure, you betcha" and you didn't laugh.

….Everyone you know has a cabin.

….You get sick of people asking you where Paisley Park is.

….You know that Lake Wobegon isn't real and you know who made it up.

….You don't understand the concept of merging or staying in your own lane.

You Might Be A Redneck Jedi If....

....You ever heard the phrase, "May the force be with y'all."

....Your Jedi robe is camouflage.

....You have ever used your light saber to open a bottle of Bud.

....At least one wing of your X-Wings is primer colored.

....You can easily describe the taste of an Ewok.

....You have ever had a land-speeder up on blocks in your yard.

....The worst part of spending time on Dagobah is the dadgum skeeters.

....Wookies are offended by your B.O.

....You have ever used the force to get yourself another beer so you didn't have to wait for a commercial.

....You have ever used the force in conjunction with fishing/bowling.

....Your father has ever said to you, "Shoot, son comon over to the dark side; it'll be a hoot."

....You have ever had your R-2 unit use its self-defense electro-shock thingy to get the barbecue grill to light.

....You have a confederate flag painted on the hood of your land-speeder.

....You ever fantasized about Princess Leah wearing Daisy Duke shorts.

....You have the doors of your X-wing welded shut and you have to get in through the window.

....Although you had to kill him, you kinda thought that Jabba the Hutt had a pretty good handle on how to treat his women.

....You have a cousin who bears a strong resemblance to Chewbacca.

....You suggested that they outfit the Millennium Falcon with a redwood deck.

....You were the only person drinking Jack Daniels during the cantina scene.

....You hear . . . "Luke, I am your father ... and your uncle ..."

Top 30 Signs You've Joined A Cheap HMO

30. Enema? The lavatory faucet swivels to face upward.
29. Costly MRI equipment efficiently replaced by an oversized 2-sided copier.
28. 24-hour claims line is 1-800-TUF-LUCK.
27. Your "primary care physician" is wearing the pants you gave to goodwill last month.
26. You can get your flu shot as soon as THE hypodermic needle is dry.
25. Recycled bandages.
24. Thermometers are too expensive so the doctor just French kisses you.
23. Preprinted prescription pads that say, "Walk it off you sissy."
22. Plan covers only "group" gynecological exams.
21. Only Proctologist in the plan is "Gus" from Roto-Rooter.
20. Only participating physicians are Dr. Fine, Dr. Howard, Dr. Fine.
19. Only item listed under Preventive Care feature of coverage is "an apple a day."
18. Doctor listens to your heart through a paper towel tube.
17. Directions to your doctor's office included, "take a left when you enter the trailer park."
16. Chief Surgeon graduated from University of Benihana.
15. "Pre-natal vitamin" prescription is a box of Tic-Tacs.
14. Radiation treatment for cancer patients requires them to walk around with a postcard from Chernobyl in their pocket.
13. Covered postnatal care consists of leaving your baby on Mia Farrow's doorstep.
12. Tongue depressors taste faintly of Fudgesickle.
11. The company logo features a hand squeezing a bleeding turnip.
10. "Take two leaches and call me in the morning."
9. Tight budget prevents acquisition of separate rectal thermometers.
8. "Will you be paying in eggs or pelts?"
7. You swear you saw salad tongs and a crab fork on the instrument tray just before the anesthesia kicked in.
6. Exam room has a tip jar.
5. Annual breast exam conducted at Hooters.
4. You ask for Viagra. You get a Popsicle stick and duct tape.
3. Head-wound victim in the waiting room is on the last chapter of "War and Peace."
2. Use of antibiotics deemed an "unauthorized experimental procedure."

AND, the Number One sign you've joined a cheap HMO…..

1. Pedal-powered dialysis machines.

The Five Stages Of Drunkenness

Stage 1 - SMART

This is when you suddenly become an expert on every subject in the known universe. You know you know everything and want to pass on your knowledge to anyone who will listen. At this stage you are always RIGHT. And, of course, the person you are talking to is very WRONG. This makes for an interesting argument when both parties are SMART.

Stage 2 - GOOD LOOKING

This is when you realize that you are the BEST LOOKING person in the entire bar and that people like you. You can go up to a perfect stranger knowing they like you and really want to talk to you. Bear in mind that you are still SMART, so you can talk to this person about any subject under the sun.

Stage 3 - RICH

This is when you suddenly become the richest person in the world. You can buy drinks for the entire bar because you have an armored truck full of money parked behind the bar. You can also make bets at this stage, because of course, you are still SMART, so naturally you win all your bets. It doesn't matter how much you bet 'cos you are RICH. You will also buy drinks for everyone that you like, because now you are the RICHEST, BEST LOOKING person in the world.

Stage 4 - BULLET PROOF

You are now ready to pick fights with anyone and everyone especially those with whom you have been betting or arguing. This is because nothing can hurt you. At this point, you can also go up to the partners of the people who you like and challenge to a battle of wits or money. You have no fear of losing this battle because you are SMART, you are RICH and hell, you're BETTER LOOKING than they are anyway!

Stage 5 - INVISIBLE

This is the Final Stage of Drunkenness. At this point, you can do anything because NO ONE CAN SEE YOU. You dance on a table to impress the people who you like because the rest of the people in the room cannot see you. You are also invisible to the person who wants to fight you. You can walk through the street singing at the top of your lungs because no one can see or hear you, and because you're still SMART, you know all the words.

Assicons

We all know those cute little computer symbols called "emoticons," where :) means a smile and :(is a frown. Sometimes these are represented by :-) and :-(respectively. Well, how about some "assicons?"   Here's how it goes:

(_!_)   a regular ass

(__!__)   a fat ass

(!)   a tight ass

(_._)   a flat ass

(_!__)   a lop-sided ass

(_x_)   kiss my ass

(_X_)   keep of my ass

(_zzz_)   a lazy ass

(_o^o_)   a wise ass

(_E=3Dmc2_)   a smart ass

(_13_)   an unlucky ass

(_$_)   Money coming out of his ass

(_?_)   Dumb Ass

You Know You Drink Too Much Coffee When....

Juan Valdez named his donkey after you.

You ski uphill.

You get a speeding ticket even when you're parked.

You speed walk in your sleep.

You have a bumper sticker that says, "Coffee drinkers are good in the sack."

You answer the door before people knock.

You haven't blinked since the last lunar eclipse.

You just completed another sweater and you don't know how to knit.

You grind your coffee beans in your mouth.

You sleep with your eyes open.

You have to watch videos in fast-forward.

The only time you're standing still is during an earthquake.

You can take a picture of yourself from ten feet away without using the timer.

You lick your coffeepot clean.

You spend every vacation visiting "Maxwell House."

You're the employee of the month at the local coffeehouse and you don't even work there.

You've worn out your third pair of tennis shoes this week.

Your eyes stay open when you sneeze.

You chew on other people's fingernails.

The nurse needs a scientific calculator to take your pulse.

You're so jittery that people use your hands to blend their margaritas.

You can type sixty words per minute with your feet.

You can jump-start your car without cables.

Cocaine is a downer.

All your kids are named "Joe."

You don't need a hammer to pound in nails.

Your only source of nutrition comes from "Sweet & Low."

You don't sweat, you percolate.

You buy milk by the barrel.

You've worn out the handle on your favorite mug.

You go to AA meetings just for the free coffee.

You walk twenty miles on your treadmill before you realize it's not plugged in.

You forget to unwrap candy bars before eating them.

You've built a miniature city out of little plastic stirrers.

People get dizzy just watching you.

When you find a penny, you say, "Find a penny, pick it up. Ninety-four more, I'll have a cup."

You've worn the finish off your coffee table.

The Taster's Choice couple wants to adopt you.

Starbucks owns the mortgage on your house.

Your taste buds are so numb you could drink your lava lamp.

You're so wired, you pick up FM radio.

<u>You Know You Drink Too Much Coffee When....continued</u>

Instant coffee takes too long.
You channel surf faster without a remote.
When someone says, "How are you?" You say, "Good to the last drop."
You want to be cremated just so you can spend the rest of eternity in a coffee can.
You want to come back as a coffee mug in your next life.
Your birthday is a national holiday in Brazil.
You'd be willing to spend time in a Turkish prison.
You go to sleep just so you can wake up and smell the coffee.
You're offended when people use the word "brew" to mean beer.
You name your cats "Cream" and "Sugar."
You get drunk just so you can sober up.
You speak perfect Arabic without ever taking a lesson.
Your Thermos is on wheels.
Your lips are permanently stuck in the sipping position.
You have a picture of your coffee mug on your coffee mug.
You can outlast the Energizer bunny.
You short out motion detectors.
You have a conniption over spilled milk.
You don't even wait for the water to boil anymore.
Your nervous twitch registers on the Richter scale.
You think being called a "drip" is a compliment.
You don't tan, you roast.
You don't get mad, you get steamed.
Your three favorite things in life are...coffee before and coffee after.
Your lover uses soft lights, romantic music, and a glass of iced coffee to get you in the mood.
You can't even remember your second cup.
You help your dog chase its tail.
You soak your dentures in coffee overnight.
Your coffee mug is insured by Lloyds of London.
You introduce your spouse as your "Coffeemate."
You think CPR stands for "Coffee Provides Resuscitation."
Your first-aid kit contains two pints of coffee with an I.V. hookup.
People can test their batteries in your ears.
Your life's goal IS to "amount to a hill of beans."

<u>Top 28 Ways You Know You're Out Of College</u>

28. Your salary is less than your tuition.
27. Your potted plants stay alive.
26. Shacking in a twin-sized bed seems absurd.
25. You keep more food than beer in the fridge.
24. You have to pay your own credit card bill.
23. Mac & Cheese no longer counts as a well-balanced meal.
22. You haven't seen a soap opera in over a year.
21. 8:00 a.m. is not early.
20. You have to file for your own taxes.
19. You hear your favorite song on the elevator at work.
18. You're not carded anymore.
17. You carry an umbrella.
16. You learn that "Bachelor" is nicer term for a jackass.
15. "Twenty-something" means over-qualified, under-paid and not married.
14. Your friends marry and divorce instead of hook-up and break-up.
13. You start watching the weather channel.
12. Jeans and baseball caps aren't staples in your wardrobe.
11. You can no longer take shots, and smoking gives you a sinus attack.
10. You go from 130 days of vacation time to 7.
9. You stop confusing 401K plan with 10K run.
8. You go to parties that the police don't raid.
7. Adults feel comfortable telling jokes about sex in front of you.
6. You don't know what time Wendy's closes anymore.
5. Your car insurance goes down.
4. You refer to college students as kids.
3. You drink wine, scotch and martinis instead of beer, bourbon and rum.
2. Your parents start making casual remarks about grandchildren.

AND, the Number One way you know you're out of college.....

1. You feed your dog Science Diet instead of Taco Bell and beer.

The Real Meaning Behind The Abbreviations In Women's Online Dating Ads

```
40-ish....................48
Adventurer.............Has had more partners than you ever will
Athletic.................Flat-chested
Average looking.......Ugly
Beautiful...............Pathological liar
Contagious Smile......Bring your penicillin
Educated...............College dropout
Emotionally Secure...Medicated
Feminist................Fat; ball buster
Free spirit..............Substance user
Friendship first........Trying to live down reputation as slut
Fun....................Annoying
Gentle.................Comatose
Good Listener.........Borderline Autistic
New-Age..............All body hair, all the time
Old-fashioned.........Lights out, missionary position only
Open-minded..........Desperate
Outgoing..............Loud
Passionate.............Loud
Poet...................Depressive Schzophrenic
Professional...........Real Witch
Redhead...............Shops the Clairol section
Reubenesque..........Grossly Fat
Romantic..............Looks better by candle light
Voluptuous...........Very Fat
Weight proportional to height............Hugely Fat
Wants Soulmate.......One step away from stalking
Widow..................Nagged first husband to death
Young at heart.........Toothless crone
```

The Real Meaning Behind The Abbreviations In Men's Online Dating Ads

40-ish...................52 and looking for 25-yr old
Athletic.................Sits on the couch and watches ESPN
Average looking......Unusual hair growth on ears, nose, & back
Educated..............Will always treat you like an idiot
Free Spirit.............Sleeps with your sister
Friendship first........As long as friendship involves nudity
Fun......................Good with a remote and a six pack
Good looking..........Arrogant
Honest.................Pathological Liar
Huggable...............Overweight, more body hair than a bear
Like to cuddle.........Insecure, overly dependent
Mature.................Until you get to know him
Open-minded..........Wants to sleep with your sister but she's not interested
Physically fit..........I spend a lot of time in front of mirror admiring myself
Poet.....................Has written on a bathroom stall
Spiritual................Once went to church with his grandmother on Easter Sunday
Stable..................Occasional stalker, but never arrested
Student................Unemployed
Thoughtful.............Says, "Please" when demanding a beer

Top 12 New Possible Beer Warnings

12. **WARNING**: Consumption of alcohol is a major factor in dancing like an asshole.
11. **WARNING**: Consumption of alcohol may cause you to tell the same boring story over and over again until your friends want to SMASH YOUR HEAD IN.
10. **WARNING**: Consumption of alcohol may cause you to thay shings like thish.
9. **WARNING**: Consumption of alcohol may lead you to believe that ex-lovers are really dying for you to telephone them at 4 in the morning.
8. **WARNING**: Consumption of alcohol may leave you wondering what the hell happened to your pants.
7. **WARNING**: Consumption of alcohol may cause you to roll over in the morning and see something really scary (whose species and or name you can't remember).
6. **WARNING**: Consumption of alcohol may actually CAUSE pregnancy.
5. **WARNING**: Consumption of alcohol may create the illusion that you are tougher, handsomer and smarter than some really, really big guy named Bob.
4. **WARNING**: Consumption of alcohol may lead you to believe you are invisible.
3. **WARNING**: Consumption of alcohol may lead you to think people are laughing WITH you.
2. **WARNING**: Consumption of alcohol may cause flux in the time-space continuum, whereby small (and sometimes large) gaps of time may seem to literally "disappear."

AND, the Number One possible new beer warning.....

1. **WARNING**: Consumption of alcohol is the leading cause of inexplicable rug burns on the forehead.

Top 24 Reasons You "Betcha" You're A Minnesotan

24. You've spent the last 15 minutes getting your child dressed to play in the snow only to have him tell you he has to go to POTTY NOW....
23. You know the four seasons: Winter, Still Winter, Not Winter & Almost Winter.
22. You find 40 degrees only a mite chilly.
21. When you win the prize for the smallest fish, you're proud of it.
20. You own three spices: salt, pepper, and ketchup.
19. You have more miles on your snow blower than your car.
18. You know Ole and Lena personally.
17. You design Halloween costumes to fit over snowmobile suits.
16. You feel warm and toasty at 12 degrees.
15. You know which leaves make good toilet paper.
14. Even though you're not breaking the law, you break into a cold sweat when the game warden appears.
13. You owe more money on your snowmobile than on your car.
12. You think the opening of Deer Season is a national holiday.
11. You think everyone from a different state has an accent.
10. You (or your mate) think sexy lingerie is a flannel nightgown with only eight buttons.
9. You've taken your kids trick-or-treating in a blizzard.
8. You find it exciting to stare through a hole in the ice and look at the bottom.
7. You have 10 favorite recipes for venison.
6. You can tell the difference between a gopher and a chipmunk at 300 yards.
5. You think white rice is exotic and wild rice is a hot dish.
4. You've arrived at a formal affair in your best dress suit wearing your finest jewelry and Sorrel insulated boots.
3. Somewhere in the state is a piece of metal with bits of your tongue stuck to it.
2. At least three times a year, your kitchen doubles as a meat processing plant.

And, the Number One reason you "becha" you're a Minnesotan.....

1. You thought "Grumpy Old Men" was a documentary.

<u>Top 19 Ways To Annoy Your Bathroom Stall Mate</u>

19. Drop a D cup bra under the stall wall and sing "Born Free" (works best if a male).
18. Lower a small mirror underneath the stall wall so you can see your neighbor and say "Peekaboo!"
17. Before you unroll the toilet paper, conspicuously lay down your "Cross dressers Anonymous" Newsletter on the floor visible to the adjacent stall.
16. Play a well known drum cadence over and over again on your butt cheeks.
15. Say, "Boy, that sure looks like a maggot!"
14. Say "@#$#, I knew that drain hole was a little too small. Now what am I gonna do?"
13. Say, "C'mon Mr. Happy, don't fall asleep on me now!"
12. Drop a peanut butter filled toilet paper ball under into the next stall, and say, "Whoops, can you kick that back over here?"
11. Say, "Interesting, more sinkers than floaters"
10. Fill up a large flask with mountain dew and squirt it erratically under the stall walls of your neighbor while yelling, "Whoa boy! Slow down!"
9. Say, "Now how did that get there?"
8. Say, "Humus. Reminds me of humus"
7. Grunt and strain real loud for 30 seconds and the drop a cantaloupe into the toilet from a high place and sigh relaxingly.
6. Say "d$%^ this water is cold!"
5. Drop a marble and say, "Oh *&%! My glass eye!"
4. Say "Hmm, I've never seen that color before!"
3. Cheer and clap loudly every time someone breaks the silence with a bodily function noise.
2. Say, "Uh oh, I knew I shouldn't put my lips on that."

AND, the Number One way to annoy your bathroom stall mate.....

1. Stick your palm under the stall wall and ask your neighbor, "May I borrow a highlighter?"

What Cold Means

60° Californians put their sweaters on.

50° Miami residents turn on the heat.

45° Vermont residents go to outdoor concerts.

40° You can see your breath. Californians shiver uncontrollably; Minnesotans go swimming.

35° Italian cars don't start.

32° Water freezes.

30° You plan your vacation in Australia.

25° Ohio water freezes. Californians weep pitiably. Minnesotans eat ice cream. Canadians go swimming.

20° Politicians begin to talk about the homeless. New York City water freezes. Miami residents plan vacation farther south.

15° French cars don't start. Your cat (dog) insists on sleeping in your bed with you.

10° You need jumper cables to get the car going.

5° American cars don't start.

0° Alaskans put on T-shirts.

-10° German cars don't start. Eyes freeze shut when you step outside.

-15° You can cut your breath and use it to build an igloo. People from Arkansas stick their tongue on metal objects. Miami residents cease to exist.

-20° Cat (dog) insists on sleeping in pajamas with you. Politicians actually do something about the homeless. Minnesotans shovel snow off roof. Japanese cars don't start.

-25° Too cold to think. You need jumper cables to get the driver going.

-30° You plan a two week hot bath. Swedish cars don't start.

-40° Californians disappear. Minnesotans button top button. Canadians put on sweater. Your car helps you plan your trip South.

-50° Congressional hot air freezes. Alaskans close the bathroom window.

-80° Polar bears move South. Green Bay Packer fans order hot cocoa at the game.

-90° Lawyers put their hands in their own pockets.

-100° Hell freezes over - Clinton finally tells all.

Top 10 Ways To Tell If A Redneck Has Been Working On A Computer

10. The monitor is up on blocks.

9. Outgoing faxes have tobacco stains on them.

8. The six front keys have rotted out.

7. The extra RAM slots have Dodge truck parts installed in them.

6. The numeric keypad only goes up to six.

5. The password is "Bubba."

4. The CPU has a gun rack mount.

3. There is a Skoal tin in the CD-ROM drive.

2. The keyboard is camouflaged.

AND, the Number One way to tell if a redneck has been working on a computer.....

1. The mouse is referred to as a "critter."

Great Moments In Pumpkin History

13,000 BC--The probable first jack o'lantern is carved. Discovered in 1957, outside the cave mouth at Lascaux, France, the first jack o'lantern was hardly discernible as such. Archeology student, Myron Bloomfieldt remarked, "I thought it was a pile of petrified goo. Not until I discovered what appeared to be a tiny primitive candle, did I know we were onto something here."

1543--Copernicus first proposes that a giant pumpkin is at the center of the solar system and the earth is but one of several orbiting gourds. He later recants in favor of a "helio-centered system."

c1600--Shakespeare first hums, "Peter, Peter Pumpkin-eater." Later, the bard, expands on this notion and pens, "The Taming of the Shrew."

1648--John Bunyan attempts to begins the allegorical "Pumpkin's Progress." He fails at this first attempt to preach.

1719--Isaac Newton trips and falls in his neighbor's pumpkin patch and "discovers" gravity. Later, changes the story to an apple falling on his head to "cover up my oafishness."

1912--The Titanic hits an enormous pumpkin and sinks. The Captain alters his version of the incident later because, "Who would believe me?"

1960--Charles Schultz begins "It's the Great Pumpkin, Charlie Brown!" after seeing a summerstock production of Beckett's "Waiting for Godot."

c1970's--New York Mayor Ed Koch suggests that changing the city's nickname from "The Big Apple" to "The Big Pumpkin," may turn the city's sagging economy around. Koch states, "Pumpkins are bigger than apples."

Top 10 Ways To Know If You Have PMS

10. You're sure that everyone is scheming to drive you crazy.
9. Your husband is suddenly agreeing to everything you say.
8. You're counting down the days until menopause.
7. Everyone around you has an attitude problem.
6. You're using your cellular phone to dial up every bumper sticker that says, "How's my driving call 1-800-***-****."
5. Everyone's head looks like an invitation to batting practice.
4. You're convinced there's a God and he's male.
3. The ibuprofen bottle is empty and you bought it yesterday.
2. The dryer has shrunk every last pair of your jeans.
AND, the Number One way to know if you have PMS.....
1. You're adding chocolate chips to your cheese omelet.

Top 10 Reasons God Created Eve

10. God worried that Adam would always be lost in the garden because men hate to ask for directions.
9. As the Bible says, "It is not good for man to be alone!"
8. God knew that Adam would never buy a new fig leaf when his seat wore out and would therefore need Eve to get one for him.
7. God knew that Adam would never make a doctor's appointment for himself.
6. God knew that Adam would never remember which night was garbage night.
5. God knew that if the world was to be populated, men would never be able to handle childbearing.
4. As "Keeper of the Garden," Adam would never remember where he put his tools.
3. The scripture account of creation indicates Adam needed someone to blame his troubles on when God caught him hiding in the garden.
2. God knew that Adam would one day need someone to hand him the TV remote.

AND, the Number One reason God created Eve.....

1. When God finished the creation of Adam, He stepped back, scratched His head and said, "I can do better than that."

Top 12 Things Not To Say To A Cop

12. Sorry, Officer, I didn't realize my radar detector wasn't plugged in.
11. Aren't you the guy from the Village People?
10. Hey, you must've been doin' about 125 mph to keep up with me. Good job!
9. Are You Andy or Barney?
8. I thought you had to be in relatively good physical condition to be a police officer.
7. You're not gonna check the trunk, are you?
6. I pay your salary!
5. Gee, Officer! That's terrific. The last officer only gave me a warning, too!
4. Do you know why you pulled me over? Okay, just so one of us does.
3. I was trying to keep up with traffic. Yes, I know there are no other cars around. That's how far ahead of me they are.
2. When the Officer says, "Gee Son, your eyes look red. Have you been drinking?" You probably shouldn't respond with, "Gee Officer your eyes look glazed, have you been eating doughnuts?"

AND, the Number One thing Not to say to a cop.....
1. I can't reach my license unless you hold my beer. (OK in Texas)

ABOUT THE AUTHOR

J.D. Heskin was awarded his BA in Psychology from the University of Minnesota in 1989, a BA in Health and Natural Sciences from the College of St. Scholastica in 1997, and an MA in Physical Therapy from the College of St. Scholastica in 1999. He was awarded his Doctorate of Physical Therapy degree from the College of St. Scholastica in 2009. He works for a major health care system in the upper Midwest and he has also taught for local colleges in this area as well. Writing is a side passion for him and his topics of interest range from the medical field to humor, poetry, science fiction, personal growth and inspiration. He has been published in his field in professional journals and aspires to expand his publications to a wider readership on topics of interest to the general public.

66437124R00125

Made in the USA
Charleston, SC
19 January 2017